ZAKKA HANDMADES

Amy Morinaka

Creative Publishing international

First published in the United States of America by Creative Publishing international, Inc., a member of Quayside Publishing Group
400 First Avenue North
Suite 400
Minneapolis, MN 55401
1-800-328-3895
www.creativepub.com

ISBN: 978-1-58923-750-6

10 9 8 7 6 5 4 3 2 1

Library of Congress Cataloging-in-Publication Data available

Resources

Eraser blocks for eraser stamp carving:
Kinokuniya Bookstores - www.kinokuniya.com/us/
Daiso - www.daisojapan.com/
Etsy.com - www.etsy.com/ (search for "Japanese eraser blocks")

Rubber stamps:
Cavallini & Co. - www.cavallini.com/stamps.html
TPC Studio - www.tpcstudio.com/

Fabrics, notions, and supplies:
Momen Plus (Fabric store in Torrance, CA, that specializes in Japanese fabrics and sewing supplies) - www.momenplus.com
Etsy - www.etsy.com
Purl - www.purlsoho.com
Sew Mama Sew - www.sewmamasew.com
Joann Fabric and Craft Stores - www.joann.com
Nippori Textile Town (Fabric district near Nippori station, Tokyo, Japan) – http://nippori-senigai.com

Technical Editor: Karen Manthey
Copy Editor: Catherine Broberg
Proofreader: Karen Ruth
Book Design: Laura H. Couallier, Laura Herrmann Design
Cover Design: Laura H. Couallier, Laura Herrmann Design
Illustrations: Amy Morinaka
Photographs: Glenn Scott Photography

Printed in China

CONTENTS

INTRODUCTION

Acknowledgments

I am very grateful to Ms. Linda Neubauer, who is the acquisition editor of this book, for discovering me and giving me the opportunity to write this book. You have provided straight-forward information and supportive feedback to someone who had no idea how the book is published (me). Thank you, Linda!

Thank you from the bottom of my heart to everyone at Creative Publishing international for your amazing talents and efforts to make this book become reality.

Thank you to the continuing inspirations and warm feedback I receive from the online crafting and blogging community. I can't imagine my life without all of you talented, supportive, and kind folks out there to share my passion of crafting.

Thank you to Atsuko and Yuko for your encouragement and lasting friendship.

Thank you to my mom, my sisters, brothers, and my extended family members, for your love, support, and laughter.

Lastly, I am very thankful to my husband, Ben, for your understanding in my passion and obsession of crafting. I'm so fortunate that I married a man who never complains (or even notices) about my ever growing inventory of fabric and yarn collection! And to my lovely girls, thank you for your pickiness that continues to fuel my creativity switch! I love you all.

Thank you for picking up this book! I am happy to share the joy of creating handmade zakka to add small happiness to your life. Growing up in Japan, I have always adored zakka, because Japan is a place packed with zakka! I now live in sunny California with my husband and two girls, and nothing is more fascinating than seeing how the world of handmade zakka is capturing the minds of crafters across the oceans.

So what is zakka? In Japanese, it refers to the small necessities of everyday life. It is a very broad term that includes accessories, stationery, fashion items, toys, home goods, kitchen items, small furniture, and much more. Zakka is not a form of art, but rather charming and practical items that are part of modern culture in Japan.

Handmade zakka is made by delicately combining natural fibers of 100 percent linen, cotton, and wool with small embellishments and meticulous handwork. Nature-inspired animals and flowers, houses and buildings, sewing notions, and characters from children's books—these are among the many motifs used to decorate zakka or to model the shapes of zakka. Many zakka designs are inspired by traditions and cultures from around the globe, including French country, Scandinavian natural style, Eastern European folk art, American vintage, and Asian ethnic, just to name a few.

In this book, I have combined my favorite handwork techniques of sewing, piecing patchwork, crocheting, embroidering, and carving eraser stamps to create original handmade zakka. Projects such as Sashiko-Style Coasters (page 102), Wrap-Around Chopsticks Holder (page 112), and Insulated Bento Lunch Bag (page 106) are traditional Japanese handicrafts with the added flair of modern zakka.

Gift giving becomes very special when you personalize your handmade zakka. Hand-stitch baby's initials or name to the Patchwork Bib (page 74) and use alphabet stamps or embroider recipient's name to the mailing label of Airmail Mug Rug (page 98). Or stuff the Fabric Bucket with Hangtag (page 28) with gifts and use the Hangtag as a gift tag.

Regardless of your zakka-making experience, I hope you find inspiration in this book and enjoy making the projects. They are mostly small items that can be made by following the step-by-step instructions. But remember, there is really no right or wrong way to design and create your handmade zakka—just believe in yourself and create items that make you smile.

EVERYDAY ZAKKA

Add simple pleasures to your life by creating zakka items that can be used every day. Create Fabric Buckets with Hangtags to organize your living space and Eraser Stamped Lavender Sachets for your clothes closet. Accessorize your fashions with Crochet-Edged One-Yard Scarf and Cotton Flower Bag Charm. Many of these zakka items can be made with small pieces of fabrics and supplies—make them for your friends and family as thoughtful gifts and make them for yourself as well.

ERASER STAMPED LAVENDER SACHET

Finished Size: *4½" (11.4 cm) square, not including the hanging loop*

A gently scented sachet filled with dried lavender is one of my favorite relaxing items. I embellished this sachet by stamping my hand-carved eraser stamps onto lightweight linen and framing it inside a coordinating fabric. Instead of carving your own stamp, use your favorite stamp from the local craft store. If you have difficulty stamping on linen, try using unbleached muslin instead. When stuffing dried lavender, be careful to avoid packing the lavender too firmly inside the sachet; keep it slightly loose so it will release the aroma when you squeeze it.

Adding a touch of European-inspired folk motifs and alphabet monograms is widely popular in the Japanese zakka design.

MATERIALS

Fabric:

- scrap of lightweight linen, at least 3½" (8.9 cm) square, for the center
- one fat eighth or 22" × 9" (55.9 cm × 22.9 cm) piece of cotton print, for the front frame and back

Other Supplies:

- rubber or eraser-carved stamp that fits inside the 3" (7.6 cm) square. Follow instructions (opposite) to carve your own eraser stamp.
- fabric ink pad
- 7" (17.8 cm) lace ribbon, for the hanging loop
- 10" (25.4 cm) grosgrain ribbon, ⅜" (1 cm) wide, for the bow
- dried lavender buds, approximately ⅔ cup or 20 to 30 g
- funnel (or make a paper funnel as described on page 11)
- liquid seam sealer or craft glue to seal cut ends of ribbons

Optional—If you carve your own eraser stamp:

- eraser (Japanese eraser blocks made for eraser carving work well, but regular soft erasers are fine)
- 2B pencil
- tracing paper
- sharp craft knife

CUTTING INSTRUCTIONS

- Cut 3" (7.6 cm) square from lightweight linen.
- Cut two 1½" × 3" (3.8 × 7.6 cm) strips from cotton print.
- Cut two 1½" × 5" (3.8 × 12.7 cm) strips from cotton print.
- Cut one 5" (12.7 cm) square from cotton print.

Take extra care when using the craft knife. Always point the knife away from you when carving erasers.

INSTRUCTIONS

Seam allowances are ¼" (6 mm) unless otherwise noted.

Optional: How to Carve Your Own Eraser Stamp

1. Draw your original stamp design or trace a stamp pattern from page 123 onto a piece of tracing paper using a 2B pencil. Color the inside of the traced pattern with 2B pencil.

2. Using a craft knife, cut the eraser to fit the approximate size of the pattern. Place the traced pattern facedown on the eraser surface. Scratch the tracing paper well with your fingernail to transfer the design onto the eraser.

3. Using a craft knife, begin carving the eraser along the traced pattern. When carving, tilt the knife slightly toward the *outside* of the design. Carve along the entire outer line of the traced pattern. Cut off the unwanted corners and edges of the eraser.

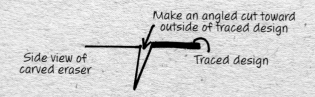

Make an angled cut toward outside of traced design

Side view of carved eraser

Traced design

4. Insert the knife at an angle in the opposite direction of the first cut to make a V-shaped cut on the eraser surface.

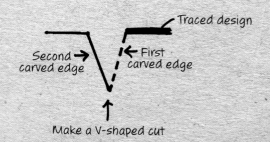

Traced design

Second carved edge

First carved edge

Make a V-shaped cut

Carve Your Own Eraser Stamp (cont.)

5. Insert the knife into the side of the eraser to cut off the unwanted edge around the carved design. The carved design should stand out from the eraser surface for stamping.

V-shaped cut around the design

6. Here are right and wrong examples of the carved eraser.

Cross section of a carved eraser

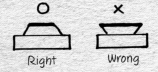

Right   Wrong

Stamp on Linen

1. Ink the stamp and stamp it onto the 3" (7.6 cm) linen square, centered. I used various colors of ink for stamping, but you can use a single color. After stamping, allow the ink to dry and heat set with a hot iron.

Tip

To put ink on your stamp, tap the fabric ink pad several times onto the stamp surface, instead of pressing the stamp onto the ink pad. This is especially helpful if your ink pad comes in a small size. Also, wipe off the unwanted ink on the edge of the stamp using cotton swabs.

Assemble the Front Panel

1. Pin and sew 1½" × 3" (3.8 × 7.6 cm) strips of cotton print to the top and bottom of the 3" (7.6 cm) linen square. Press seams away from the linen square.

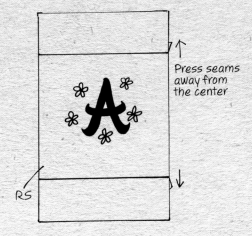

Press seams away from the center

RS

2. Pin and sew 1½" × 5" (3.8 × 12.7 cm) strips of cotton print to the right and left sides of the opposite edges to form a square. Press seams away from the center.

Press seams away from the center

3. Fold a 7" (17.8 cm) piece of lace ribbon in half widthwise to form a loop.

4. Aligning the raw edges, center the lace ribbon ends on the top edge of the right side of assembled front panel, with the loop end pointing toward the bottom of the front panel. Pin and sew in place, going back and forth to reinforce the stitches and using an 1/8" (3 mm) seam allowance.

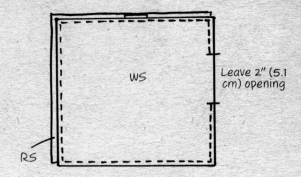

Leave 2" (5.1 cm) opening

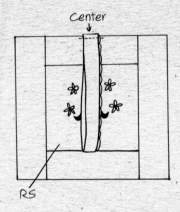

Finish the Sachet

1. With right sides facing together, pin the assembled front panel and the square back together. Sew around all four sides, leaving a 2" (5.1 cm) opening on one side. Be careful not to catch the trim's loop end when you sew. Press to open seams. Trim the four corners.

2. Turn the sachet right side out through the opening and use a chopstick to push out the corners. Press again.

3. Using a funnel, fill the sachet with dried lavender. Do not overfill. If you don't have a funnel, roll a piece of paper in a cone, and tape it together.

4. Hand-stitch the opening closed with a matching thread.

5. Tie a bow using 10" (25.4 cm) grosgrain ribbon at the bottom edge of the lace hanging. Gently pull the tails of the ribbon and cut off any excess. Dab a small amount of glue to both ribbon tails to seal the cut ends. Let dry.

6. Using matching thread, stitch through the knot to secure the ribbon in place. Be very careful when passing a needle through the knot, as you are stitching through several layers.

For Variation

This sachet is made from an upcycled pillow case and embellished with a store-bought vintage style stamp. TPC Studio's Vintage Keys Rubber Cling Stamp is used.

CROCHET-EDGED ONE-YARD SCARF

Finished Size: *9½" × 72" (24.1 × 182.8 cm)*

It takes exactly one yard (0.92 m) of fabric to make this scarf. The edgings are crocheted separately using 100 percent cotton yarn and stitched onto the ends of the scarf with a sewing machine. Only the basic crochet stitches of chains, single crochets, and double crochets are used to make the edging strips. I used the same fabric for both the front and back sides of this scarf, but you can make it reversible by using a different fabric, or combine several scraps from your favorite fabrics. For optional embellishment, stitch a small scrap piece of lettered fabric to the bottom corner of the scarf, creating an original fabric label.

This scarf incorporates both sewing and crocheting techniques into one project, a unique approach in the creation of Japanese zakka design.

MATERIALS

Fabric:

- 1 yd (0.92 m) cotton, lightweight linen, or cotton/linen blend. Yardage is based on 42" (106.7 cm) wide fabric.

- small scrap of fabric to cut out your selected word, set of alphabets or numbers, or any small motif to add fabric label embellishment to the scarf, optional

Other Supplies:

- 30 yds (27.5 m) four-ply 100% cotton yarn, in ecru, or any color to match your fabric. Sample uses Lily Sugar 'n Cream. (Yarn weight: 4 Medium)

- size 7/G (4.5 mm) crochet hook

- steam iron

CUTTING INSTRUCTIONS

- Cut four 10" × 36" (25.4 × 91.4 cm) strips from 1 yd (0.92 m) fabric following the lengthwise fabric grain. See diagram as a guide.

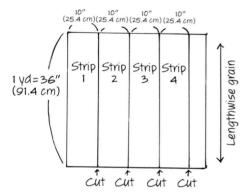

10" (25.4 cm) 10" (25.4 cm) 10" (25.4 cm) 10" (25.4 cm)

1 yd = 36" (91.4 cm)

Strip 1 | Strip 2 | Strip 3 | Strip 4

Lengthwise grain

Cut Cut Cut Cut

Tip

For easier pressing, cut out a rectangle template from firm cardboard, such as a postcard or cereal box, into your desired finished label size. Use the template to fold all four edges of the label piece inward with a hot iron.

INSTRUCTIONS

Seam allowances are ¼" (6 mm) unless otherwise noted.

Join the Scarf Pieces

1. With right sides together, pin and sew the short edges of two fabric strips to make one long strip. Press open the seams. Repeat with the remaining two fabric strips to create another long strip. Now you have two long scarf strips.

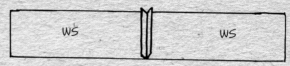

WS   WS

Sew two strips together, joining the short edges

Optional: Add your original fabric label

1. Cut out a word, a set of letters or numbers, or any small motif of your choice from print fabric scrap to create original fabric label. When you cut out the motif, leave at least a ½" (1.3 cm) seam allowance around the word or motif.

2. Fold and press the four edges of the scrap piece inward, to create a fabric label.

3. Position the label at the bottom right corner of the right side of the scarf strip. Pin the label 1½" (3.8 cm) inside from both corner edges. Pin and sew the label to the scarf using matching thread.

RS

RS

Stitch label in place 1½" (3.8 cm) from both edges

Crochet the Edging

1. Create two strips of crochet edging following the instructions and stitching diagram below. For a nice finish, steam the finished crochet edging using a steam iron. Pin the edging into desired shape on a flat ironing board. Hold steam iron several inches (cm) above the crocheted piece to steam the edging into shape.

Gauge: *Size of one crocheted edging is approximately 9½" × ½" (24.1 × 3.8 cm)*

Instructions:

Ch 45.

Row 1: Dc in 4th ch from hook and in each ch across, turn. (43 dc)

Row 2: Ch 4 (counts as dc, ch 1), skip first 2 dc, *dc in next dc, ch 1, skip next dc; rep from * across, dc in top of turning ch, turn. (22 ch-1 spaces)

Row 3: Ch 1, sc in first dc, *ch 3, skip next ch-1 space, sc in next dc; rep from * across, ending with last sc in 3rd ch of turning ch. Fasten off.

Finish the Scarf

1. With right sides together, combine the scarf strips, matching the center seams. Pin and sew around all sides, leaving at least a 4" (10.2 cm) opening along one long edge. Press to open the seams. Clip the four corners. Turn the scarf right side out through the opening and use a chopstick to push out the corners. Press again.

2. Topstitch closely around the scarf, carefully catching the opening.

3. Place crochet edging on the short edge of the front side of the scarf, which is the side the label (optional) is sewn onto. Overlap approximately ½" (1.3 cm) of the scarf's short edge and the first row of crochet edging (the entire row of double crochet). Pin and machine-stitch the crochet edging closely to the top edge using matching thread, as shown in the diagram.

Partial Stitch Diagram

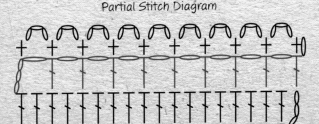

Stitch Key

- ◯ = chain
- + = single crochet
- T = double crochet

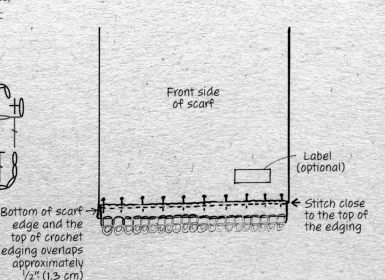

Front side of scarf

Label (optional)

Bottom of scarf edge and the top of crochet edging overlaps approximately ½" (1.3 cm)

Stitch close to the top of the edging

4. Turn the scarf over to the reverse side. Sew the crochet edging and the scarf together from the reverse side using matching thread, but this time sew over the previously topstitched line on the scarf, to secure the crochet edging. You have now topstitched two lines over the crochet edging, one from the front side and another from the reverse side. Repeat for the opposite scarf end to attach the edging.

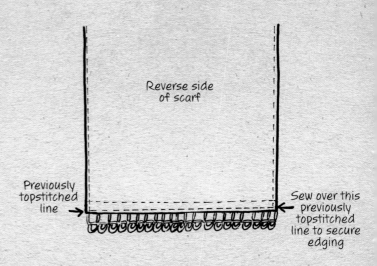

Reverse side of scarf

Previously topstitched line →

← Sew over this previously topstitched line to secure edging

For Variation

Beautiful and lightweight linen/cotton blend fabric in leaf print is used to make this scarf. For the label, I hand stamped and hand embroidered the outline of the clover motif onto a scrap of linen, and layered it on top of gingham check. Both labels' edges are folded inward and sewn close to the edges.

PATCHWORK LANYARD

Finished Size: *Approximately 36" (91.4 cm) long, or drops 18" (45.7 cm) from the back of the neck to split ring*

This lanyard, or neck strap, will make a thoughtful gift for your child's teacher, coach, medical professional, office worker, or any busy mom! It is also a great way to turn your fabric scraps into an everyday usable zakka item. Feel free to skip the rivets and leather strip attachment if you choose, though these details will surely add that zakka taste to your lanyard. The tools required to set your own rivets include ⅜" (1 cm) diameter rivet cap and bottom, small piece of soft leather, rotary leather punch, and a nylon jaw flat-nose pliers. As long as you have all tools in your hands, setting rivets is quite simple.

MATERIALS

Fabric:

- scraps of cotton print to create 2" × 36" (5.1 × 91.4 cm) strip

Other Supplies:

- strip of fusible interfacing, 1" × 35½" (2.5 × 90.2 cm). Interfacing is cut slightly shorter than the pieced strip.
- 1" (2.5 cm) split ring
- swivel hook

- ⅜" (1 cm) rivets, cap and bottom. I used a rivet bottom that is approximately ¼" (6 mm) tall.
- small strip of soft leather remnant, ½" × 2" (1.3 × 5.1 cm)
- rotary leather punch
- nylon jaw flat-nose pliers. This is a tool used for craft and jewelry making that comes with soft and protective nylon-covered jaws.
- zipper foot for your sewing machine (optional)
- pins or sewing clips, such as Clover Wonder Clips

Tip

I did not use normal rivet-setting tools, including rivet setter, anvil, and mallet, to set the rivets for this project, as I find nylon jaw flat-nose pliers more convenient. However, you may use rivet-setting tools if you choose, following the manufacturer's instructions.

For Variation

This patchwork lanyard is finished without the rivet and soft leather strip.

INSTRUCTIONS

Seam allowances are ¼" (6 mm) unless otherwise noted.

Sew the Pieced Strap

1. Cut your fabric scraps into 2" (5.1 cm) widths. Combine the pieces to create a 2" × 36" (5.1 × 91.4 cm) strip. Open all seams and press.

2. Fold the pieced 2" × 36" (5.1 × 91.4 cm) strip in half lengthwise, wrong sides together, and press. Unfold. Place a 1" × 35½" (2.5 × 90.2 cm) fusible interfacing strip over half of the wrong side of the pieced strip. Interfacing is cut slightly shorter than the pieced strip, leaving both short ends free of interfacing. Refold in half lengthwise, and press to fuse the interfacing to the wrong side of the pieced strip. Fold the long edges to meet in the center, and press again.

Tip

Instead of holding the open side of the loop together with regular pins, try using sewing clips such as Clover Wonder Clips. They are a convenient and helpful tool when holding thick fabrics together.

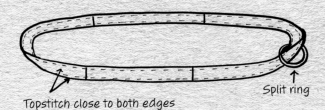

Topstitch close to both edges   Split ring

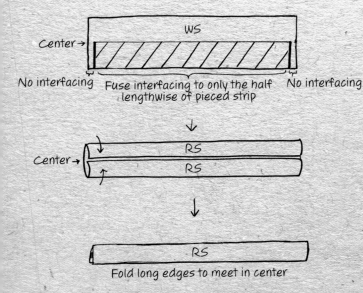

Center → WS

No interfacing Fuse interfacing to only the half lengthwise of pieced strip No interfacing

↓

Center → RS
          RS

↓

RS

Fold long edges to meet in center

3. Slip one end of the pieced strip through the split ring. With right sides together, connect the short ends of the pieced strip, being careful not to twist the strip. Sew the raw ends together to form a loop. Pin and topstitch along both edges of the loop, stitching ⅛" (3 mm) from the edges. (If you forget to slip the strip through the split ring before sewing into a loop, it's okay. Simply open the split ring and attach it onto the loop.)

4. Move the split ring around the loop to the desired location. This step is important because the fabric close to the ring (and the rivets) will be most visible when the lanyard is worn. Once the rivet position is set, topstitch across two layers of the lanyard, as close to the split ring as possible. It may be helpful to change your machine foot to zipper foot. If you do not plan to attach rivets, your lanyard is now finished. Simply attach the swivel hook to the split ring.

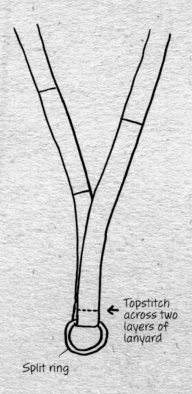

Topstitch across two layers of lanyard

Split ring

Finish the Lanyard

1. Prepare the soft leather strip. Mark two rivet points on the right side of a ½" × 2" (1.3 × 5.1 cm) soft leather strip with a pencil, ¼" (6 mm) from each short edge, centered. Wrap the connected end of the lanyard with the soft leather strip, right side facing out. Select the hole size of the rotary leather punch that best fits the diameter of the rivet shaft. (I used the smallest hole of the rotary leather punch.) At the marked rivet point, punch through the two layers of soft leather and two layers of lanyard, at once.

2. Connect all punched holes and insert the rivet cap and rivet bottom from each side of the hole. Using nylon jaw flat-nose pliers, firmly hold rivets from both sides to set in place. Attach a swivel hook to the split ring.

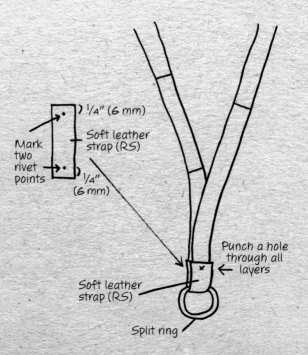

¼" (6 mm)

Soft leather strap (RS)

Mark two rivet points

¼" (6 mm)

Punch a hole through all layers

Soft leather strap (RS)

Split ring

RICE THERAPY EYE PILLOW

Finished Size: *8½" × 5" (21.6 × 12.7 cm)*

This eye pillow is filled with uncooked Japanese dry rice. Heat it in the microwave for hot therapy, or place it in a zipper plastic bag and then into a freezer for cold therapy. Use it at bedtime and the embroidered sleepy sheep on the front panel may help put you to sleep. You may replace dry rice with flaxseeds or dry adzuki beans and add lavender buds or essential oils for aromatherapy. The rice filling is kept securely inside the inner muslin bag, and the outer case has an envelope back closure that is removable and washable. Do not overheat the eye pillow in the microwave, and be careful to avoid letting the rice filling become wet.

MATERIALS

Fabric:

- 1 fat eighth or 22" × 9" (55.9 × 22.9 cm) checkered print, for the front frame and back
- 1 fat eighth or 22" × 9" (55.9 × 22.9 cm) floral print, for the front frame and back
- small scrap linen, at least 8" × 4" (20.3 × 10.2 cm), to piece the outer bag
- scrap unbleached muslin, at least 11" (27.9 cm) square, for the inner pillow

Other Supplies:

- dry rice, approximately ¾ cup (160 g)
- dried lavender buds, optional
- funnel, optional
- embroidery floss or pearl cotton thread
- pattern transfer paper, optional
- water-soluble pen, optional
- black permanent marker, optional
- masking tape, optional
- pinking shears, optional

Rice is the primary crop in Japan. Japanese rice is short grain and when cooked has a sticky texture. Cooked steamy rice with a hot miso soup is a comfort food for many Japanese people.

CUTTING INSTRUCTIONS

- Cut one 7" × 3½" (17.8 × 8.9 cm) rectangle from the linen.

- Cut two 7" × 1½" (17.8 × 3.8 cm) strips from the checkered print.

- Cut one 6" × 5½" (15.2 × 14 cm) rectangle from the checkered print.

- Cut two 5½" × 1½" (14 × 3.8 cm) strips from the floral print.

- Cut one 6" × 5½" (15.2 × 14 cm) rectangle from the floral print.

- Cut two 8¾" × 5¼" (22.2 × 13.3 cm) rectangles from the unbleached muslin.

The envelope back closure makes it easy to remove and wash the eye pillow cover. The rice filling is secured inside the inner muslin bag.

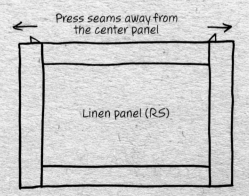

INSTRUCTIONS

Seam allowances are ¼" (6 mm) unless otherwise noted.

Assemble the Front Panel

1. Pin and sew 7" × 1½" (17.8 × 3.8 cm) strips of checkered print to the top and bottom of the linen panel. Press seams away from the linen panel.

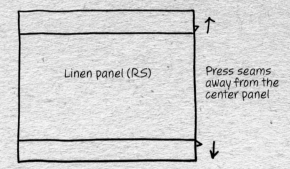

Linen panel (RS)

Press seams away from the center panel

2. Pin and sew 5½" × 1½" (14 × 3.8 cm) strips of floral print to the right and left sides of the pieced panel. Press seams away from the linen panel.

Press seams away from the center panel

Linen panel (RS)

3. Trim the pieced panel to 9" × 5½" (22.9 × 14 cm).

Transfer and Embroider the Sheep Pattern

1. Trace the embroidery design on page 126 to the bottom right corner of the front linen panel, approximately ½" (1.3 cm) from the corner edges. Use the pattern transfer paper, following the manufacturer's instructions, or refer to step 1 of Transfer and Embroider Sashiko Design on Sashiko-Style Coasters (page 104) for the Sunny Window method. With this method, design is transferred using a marker, masking tape, and water-soluble pen with the sunlight from the window.

2. Embroider the pattern onto the linen panel with embroidery floss or pearl cotton thread, using backstitches.

Finish the Outer Case

1. Create a double-folded hem on one short edge of each back piece. Fold and press one short edge of the 6" × 5½" (15.2 × 14 cm) checkered print piece, forming a ½" (1.3 cm) seam. Then press under another ¼" (6 mm) inward to create a double-folded hem. Pin and topstitch in place from the wrong side. Repeat for the 6" × 5½" (15.2 × 14 cm) floral print piece.

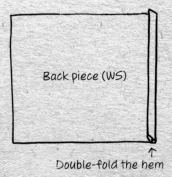

Back piece (WS)

↑
Double-fold the hem

2. With right sides together, place the back pieces over the front, overlapping them approximately 1½" (3.8 cm) at the center. Pin and sew around all four edges. Use pinking shears to cut off excess seam around the edges, to prevent fraying (optional). Turn right side out and push out corners using a chopstick. Press.

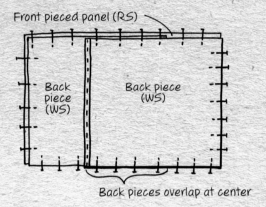

Front pieced panel (RS)

Back piece (WS)

Back piece (WS)

Back pieces overlap at center

Assemble the Inner Pillow

1. Align and pin two 8¾" × 5¼" (22.2 × 13.3 cm) muslin rectangles together, and sew around all four edges leaving at least a 2" (5.1 cm) opening on one side. Clip all corners. Turn the pillow right side out through the opening and push out the corners using a chopstick.

2. Using a funnel, insert dry rice through the opening. If you don't have a funnel, create your own by rolling a piece of paper into a cylinder shape and taping it together. Add a few spoons of lavender buds (optional), according to your preference. Machine-stitch close to the edge to close the opening.

3. Insert the inner pillow inside the outer case.

MATRYOSHKA DOLL KEY COVER

Finished Size: *3" × 3½" (7.6 × 8.9 cm), not including the cords*

I designed this key cover from the love of matryoshka, or Russian nesting dolls. This key cover is fully lined with lightweight batting and linen, and the cushioned cover prevents your keys from scratching other items in your purse, such as your cell phone. A split key ring placed inside the key cover holds the keys, and the keys can easily be pulled down to use. The doll's face is machine appliquéd onto the exterior front cover and her eyes and mouth are hand-stitched with care. Add jacquard ribbons, lace trims, cotton tapes, or ricrac trims to embellish the dress of the matryoshka.

MATERIALS

Fabric:

- small scrap of red and white gingham check print, 8" × 5" (20.3 × 12.7 cm), for the exterior
- small scrap of linen, 12" × 5" (30.5 × 12.7 cm) for the lining and face
- small scrap or 2" (5.1 cm) square of cotton print for hair

Other Supplies:

- one or two 4" (10.2 cm) length trims of various widths to embellish the front panel
- 1" (2.5 cm) diameter split key ring
- 14" (35.6 cm) length of 1 mm or 2 mm waxed cotton cord, color of choice
- one round wood bead, 12 mm in diameter
- batting, 8" × 5" (20.3 × 12.7 cm)
- lightweight paper-backed fusible web, such as HeatnBond Lite, at least 5" (12.7 cm) square to fuse face and hair

- machine sewing threads to match the color of face, hair, and the ribbon trims
- embroidery floss or pearl cotton thread to embroider eyes and mouth
- pencil
- water-soluble pen
- basting spray, optional
- cotton swab to wipe off marks from water-soluble pen, optional

CUTTING INSTRUCTIONS

- Trace the patterns on page 122 to make templates for the key cover, face and hair.
- Cut two key cover panels from the red and white gingham check print using the key cover template.
- Cut two key cover panels from the linen using the key cover template.
- Cut one 3" (7.6 cm) square from the linen.
- Cut one 2" (5.1 cm) square from the cotton print.
- Cut two panels from the batting using the key cover template.

INSTRUCTIONS

Seam allowances are ¼" (6 mm) unless otherwise noted.

Embroider the Face

1. Following the fusible web manufacturer's instructions, iron the paper-backed fusible web onto the *wrong* side of the 3" (7.6 cm) linen square.

2. Trace the outline of the face template onto the paper side of the fused linen square with a pencil. Do not trace the eyes and mouth. Cut out the face and peel off the paper backing.

3. Arrange the face onto the right side of the exterior panel, at least ½" (1.3 cm) from the top edge, centered. Press and fuse in place.

4. Based on the diagram, draw eyes and a mouth on the bottom half of the linen face using the water-soluble pen. Embroider the eyes and mouth using embroidery floss or pearl cotton thread. Use satin stitches for the eyes, and use backstitches for the eyelashes and the mouth. (See step 2 on page 80 for instructions on satin stitching. See step 2 on page 47 for instructions on backstitching.) Wet a cotton swab (optional) with few drops of water and dab over the marked lines of the water-soluble pen. Let dry.

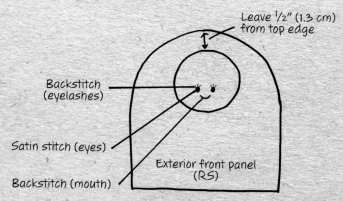

Leave ½" (1.3 cm) from top edge

Backstitch (eyelashes)

Satin stitch (eyes)

Exterior front panel (RS)

Backstitch (mouth)

Assemble the Exterior Panels

1. Spray-baste or pin the batting to the wrong sides of both the front and back exterior panels.

2. Using the matching colored sewing thread, topstitch twice around the doll's face, approximately ⅛" (3 mm) from the edge.

3. Just as you did with the doll's face, iron the paper-backed fusible web onto the *wrong* side of the 2" (5.1 cm) print square to create hair. Trace the hair template onto the paper side of the fused print using a pencil. Cut out the hair and peel off the paper backing.

4. Change the sewing machine thread to match the color of the hair. Place the hair on top of the face, centered, aligning the top edges. Press and fuse in place using a tip of the iron. Topstitch twice around the hair close to the edge.

5. Arrange the trims on the right side of the front panel, right below the face. Pin the trims in place, leaving at least ½" (1.3 cm) from the bottom edge. Using matching colored sewing threads, sew along the long edges of the trims.

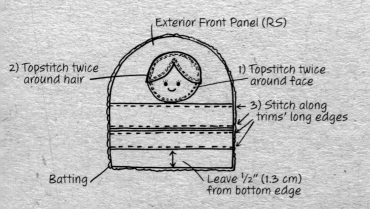

Exterior Front Panel (RS)

2) Topstitch twice around hair

1) Topstitch twice around face

3) Stitch along trims' long edges

Batting

Leave ½" (1.3 cm) from bottom edge

Assemble the Key Cover

1. With right sides together, pin the exterior panel and the lining at the top edge. Sew along the top edge. Open the seams and press. Repeat with the remaining exterior and lining panels.

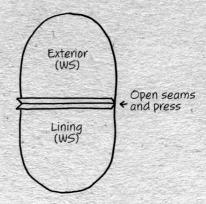

Exterior (WS)

Open seams and press

Lining (WS)

2. Place the front and back right sides together. Pin and sew around the pieces, leaving ½" (1.3 cm) cord openings at top and bottom center for both sides and 1½" (3.8 cm) opening on the lining for turning. Open seams and press. Cut notches around the curves, taking care not to cut the seam.

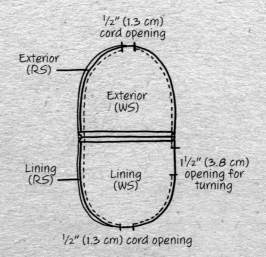

½" (1.3 cm) cord opening

Exterior (RS)

Exterior (WS)

Lining (RS)

Lining (WS)

1½" (3.8 cm) opening for turning

½" (1.3 cm) cord opening

3. Turn the key cover right side out through the opening in the lining. Hand-stitch or machine-stitch the opening of the lining closed.

4. Insert the lining inside the exterior cover. Push out corners and edges using a chopstick. Fold under the outer fabric and lining at the top opening and hand-stitch the folds together.

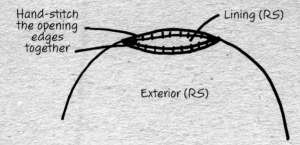

Hand-stitch the opening edges together

Lining (RS)

Exterior (RS)

Pass Cords and Finish the Key Cover

1. Fold the cord in half to make a loop and match both raw ends together. Pass the loop end of the cord through the top opening into the lining. Fasten a split key ring to the loop end.

2. Pull both ends of the cord and thread through the wood bead. Tie the cord ends together securely. Cut off the excess cords.

Tie cord ends together

Wood bead

Exterior (RS)

Lining (RS)

1" (2.5 cm) split ring

FABRIC BUCKET WITH HANGTAG

Large Size: *11½" diameter × 12¼" height (29.2 cm diameter × 31.1 cm height)*
Medium Size: *9½" diameter × 11¼" height (24.1 cm diameter × 28.6 cm height)*

Make these oversized fabric buckets in two different sizes to match any room of your house for organization and display. Or, stuff the bucket with baby items, children's toys, or craft supplies to make a practical gift presentation. Select medium- to heavyweight cotton or home decor–weight fabric for the bucket's exterior. For the lining, use double-sided pre-quilted fabric for durability and to hold its shape. Look around your kitchen to find a dinner plate, cake pan, cooking pot, mixing bowl, or any round items that are 10" (25.4 cm) and 12" (30.5 cm) diameter. They will be used as templates to trace circles for the bucket bottoms. Create matching hangtags using remnants for easy labeling of contents or to use as gift tags for a personalized touch.

MATERIALS

Fabric:

- ¾ yd (0.69 m) medium-to heavyweight cotton or home décor–weight fabric
- ¾ yd (0.69 m) double-sided pre-quilted fabric
- Note about fabrics: The fabric required is the same for the large and medium buckets and is based on 42" (106.7 cm) wide fabric.

Other Supplies:

- fusible interfacing, 20" × 8" (50.8 × 20.3 cm), to make handles
- 12" (30.5 cm) dinner plate, cake pan, cooking pot, mixing bowl, or any round item to use as template for the *large* bucket bottom
- 10" (25.4 cm) dinner plate, cake pan, cooking pot, mixing bowl or any round item to use as template for the *medium* bucket bottom
- water-soluble pen, optional
- pins or sewing clips, such as Clover Wonder Clips

CUTTING INSTRUCTIONS

For Large Bucket:

- Cut one 37¾" × 13" (95.9 × 33 cm) rectangle from medium- to heavyweight cotton or home décor fabric, for exterior panel.
- Cut one 12" diameter (30.5 cm) circle from medium- to heavyweight cotton or home décor fabric using 12" (30.5 cm) dinner plate, cooking pot, pans, or bowl as template.
- Cut two 10" × 4" (25.4 × 10.2 cm) strips from medium- to heavyweight cotton or home décor fabric, for handles.
- Cut one 37¾" × 12¾" (95.9 × 32.4 cm) rectangle from double-sided pre-quilted fabric, for lining.
- Cut one 12" (30.5 cm) diameter circle from double-sided pre-quilted fabric using 12" (30.5 cm) dinner plate, cooking pot, pans, or bowl as template.

CUTTING
INSTRUCTIONS (cont.)

For Medium Bucket:

- Cut one 31½" × 12" (80 × 30.5 cm) rectangle from medium- to heavyweight cotton or home décor fabric, for exterior panel.

- Cut one 10" diameter (25.4 cm) circle from medium- to heavyweight cotton or home décor fabric using 10" (25.4 cm) dinner plate, cooking pot, pan, or bowl as template.

- Cut two 10" × 4" (25.4 × 10.2 cm) strips from medium- to heavyweight cotton or home décor fabric for handles.

- Cut one 31½" × 11¾" (80 × 29.9 cm) rectangle from double-sided pre-quilted fabric, for lining.

- Cut one 10" diameter (25.4 cm) circle from double-sided pre-quilted fabric using 10" (25.4 cm) dinner plate, cooking pot, pan, or bowl as template.

For Both Sizes:

- Cut two 10" × 4" (25.4 × 10.2 cm) strips from interfacing.

Tip

The length (or height) of the lining is cut ¼" (6 mm) shorter than the exterior so the lining will fit smoothly inside the bucket exterior.

INSTRUCTIONS

Seam allowances are ¼" (6 mm) unless otherwise noted. The steps are the same regardless of the bucket size.

Assemble the Exterior

1. With right sides together, fold the exterior panel in half widthwise and sew the short edges together. Press to open side seam. You have sewn the exterior panel into a tube.

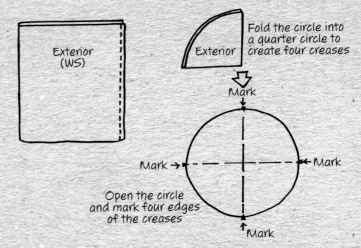

2. Fold the exterior circle into a quarter circle, creating four creases. You can do this by folding the circle in half and then folding it over again in half. Open the circle and mark all edges of the creases using a water-soluble pen (optional) or by cutting small notches with a scissor tip.

3. Create four even creases on the bottom edge of the exterior tube that you created in step 1. Using a water-soluble pen (optional) or by cutting small notches with a scissor tip, make four equal marks around the tube's bottom edge. With right sides together, match the marks on the circle with the marks on the tube edge, aligning the raw edges. Pin the four quarter sections together. Continue to pin around the bottom edge of the circle by filling between these four pins.

4. Sew around the entire circle. Go slowly and stop often, and rotate the fabric around the pivot as you go. After stitching, cut small notches around the entire outer edge of the circle, taking care not to cut the seam. Now you have sewn the exterior bucket with a round bottom.

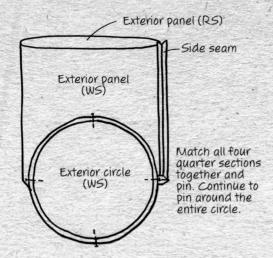

Exterior panel (RS)

Side seam

Exterior panel (WS)

Exterior circle (WS)

Match all four quarter sections together and pin. Continue to pin around the entire circle.

Assemble the Lining

1. With right sides together, fold the lining panel in half widthwise and sew the short edges together, just as you did with the exterior panel. However, this time leave a 4" (10.2 cm) opening along the edge. You have sewn the lining panel into a tube.

2. Repeat steps 2 to 4 of Assemble the Exterior to sew the lining circle and the lining tube ends together. Cut notches around the outer edge of the circle, taking care not to cut the seam. Now you have sewn a bucket lining with a round bottom.

Make and Attach Handles

1. Fuse a 10" × 4" (25.4 × 10.2 cm) strip of heavy-weight interfacing to the entire wrong side of the 10" × 4" (25.4 × 10.2 cm) strip, following manufacturer's instructions. Fold the long edges in half lengthwise, wrong sides together, and press. Then fold long edges to meet in the center and press. Pin and topstitch ⅛" (3 mm) from both long edges. Repeat to make the remaining handle. You now have two handles that are each 10" × 1" (25.4 × 2.5 cm) long. For diagram of making the handles, see step 1 on page 48.

2. Pin both ends of the handle to the top edge of the right side of the exterior bucket, aligning the raw edges. Make sure the handle is centered with 3" (7.6 cm) between the handle ends. Machine-baste the handle ends approximately ⅛" (3 mm) from the top edge. Repeat to attach the remaining handle across from the first handle.

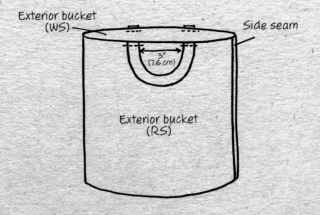

Exterior bucket (WS)

Side seam

3" (7.6 cm)

Exterior bucket (RS)

Finish the Bucket

1. With right sides together, insert the exterior bucket inside the lining and match the side seams together. Align the raw edges at the top. The handles should be sandwiched between the exterior bucket and the lining. Pin and sew around the entire top edge. Using sewing clips instead of pins may be helpful to hold the exterior and the lining together at the bucket opening.

2. Turn the bucket and the lining right side out through the opening in the lining. Hand- or machine-stitch to close the opening. Insert the lining back into the exterior and press around the opening for a clean finish. Topstitch around the upper edge of the bucket approximately ⅛" (3 mm) from the edge.

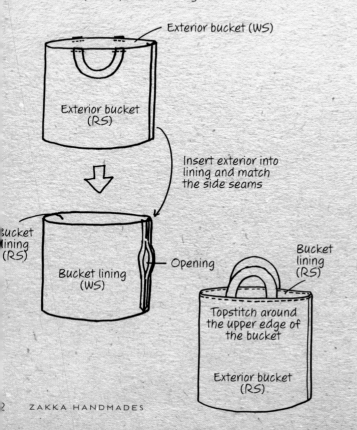

HOW TO MAKE A FABRIC HANG TAG

MATERIALS

Fabric:

- remnant scraps from making fabric bucket's exterior, at least 4" × 11" (10.2 × 27.9 cm)

Other Supplies:

- scrap of batting, at least 5" (12.7 cm) square

- piece of clear vinyl, at least 5" (12.7 cm) square. I used a heavyweight sheet protector from our office supply.

- cord, trim, ribbon, hemp, or any string to hang the tag, 11" (27.9 cm) (I used size 4.0 mm/F crochet hook and Lily Sugar 'n Cream 100% four-ply cotton yarn in Ecru to create 11" [27.9 cm] long crochet chain cord.)

- rotary cutter, optional

- basting spray, optional

- sewing clips (such as Clover Wonder Clips) or other sewing clips or clothespins to hold vinyl and fabrics together

- business card or hard paper cut into 3½" × 2" (8.9 × 5.1 cm) rectangle, to place inside the hangtag for labeling

CUTTING INSTRUCTIONS

- Cut two 3½" × 5" (8.9 × 12.7 cm) rectangles from bucket exterior fabric remnants.

- Cut one 3½" × 5" (8.9 × 12.7 cm) rectangle from batting.

- Cut one 2½" × 4" (6.4 × 10.2 cm) rectangle from clear vinyl.

INSTRUCTIONS

Seam allowances are ¼" (6 mm) unless otherwise noted.

Make the Fabric Hangtag

1. Spray-baste or pin the batting to the wrong side of one 3½" × 5" (8.9 cm × 12.7 cm) rectangle. This will be the front panel of the hangtag.

2. Fold the 11" (27.9 cm) string in half. Aligning raw edges, center the string ends on one short edge of the right side of the front panel. Pin and sew in place ⅛" (3 mm) from the edge, going back and forth to reinforce the stitches.

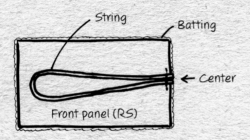

String · Batting · Center · Front panel (RS)

3. With right sides together, pin the front and back panels together. Sew around all four sides, leaving a 2" (5.1 cm) opening on one long side. Backstitch over the string ends for reinforcement. Be careful not to catch the string's loop end while you sew. Trim the corners and press the seams open.

4. Turn the hangtag right side out through the opening. Use a chopstick to push out the corners. Press again. Hand-stitch to close the opening.

5. Place the 2½" × 4" (6.4 × 10.2 cm) clear vinyl rectangle on top of the front side of the hangtag, centered. Use sewing clips or clothespins to hold the vinyl in place; do not use regular pins, as they will punch holes in the vinyl. Stitch all three sides close to the edges, using approximately ⅛" (3 mm) seam allowances and leaving the opening unsewn. Backstitch a few times at the beginning and end for reinforcement. Write or stamp words on the back side of the business card and place it inside the finished hangtag.

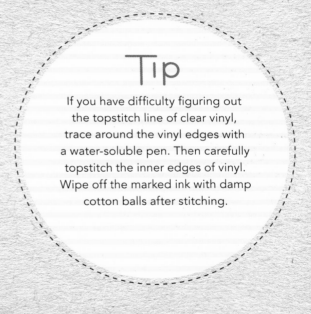

Tip

If you have difficulty figuring out the topstitch line of clear vinyl, trace around the vinyl edges with a water-soluble pen. Then carefully topstitch the inner edges of vinyl. Wipe off the marked ink with damp cotton balls after stitching.

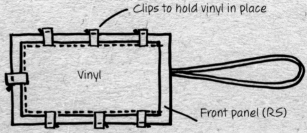

Clips to hold vinyl in place · Vinyl · Front panel (RS)

COTTON FLOWER
BAG CHARM

Finished Size: *Approximately 3" × 8" (7.6 × 20.3 cm) long, not including the chains*

Dress up your bag with this sweet crocheted flower charm. The crocheted flower is worked into triple layers using cotton yarns, and a matching covered button is placed in the center of the flower. Pieces of trims and leather strips embellish the flower charm. Sew a Simple Linen Tote to create a coordinating bag set (see page 68) or accessorize the bag you have in hand. Metal chains are attached to the back side of the charm for hanging, but you can affix a brooch pin back to create a corsage or add a split ring to use as a key ring.

MATERIALS

Fabric:

- small scrap of cotton print, at least 2" (5.1 cm) square, to make the covered button
- small scrap of batting, at least 1" (2.5 cm) square, to wrap the metal button shell, optional

Other Supplies:

- 20 yd (18.5 m) four-ply 100% cotton yarn. Sample uses Lily Sugar 'n Cream in Ecru. (Yarn weight: 4 Medium)
- size 7/G (4.5 mm) crochet hook
- tapestry needle
- two to three kinds of trim, such as lace, pompoms, and ribbon, for embellishment, each at least 14" (35.6 cm) long
- one leather strip, at least 14" (35.6 cm) long
- one size 36 or ⅞" (2.2 cm) covered button and kit
- strong thread
- metal chain, 4" (10.2 cm) long, antique gold, brass, or bronze
- metal clasp, antique gold, brass, or bronze
- jump ring, 10 mm or larger, antique gold, brass, or bronze color
- two jewelry pliers
- fabric glue, optional

INSTRUCTIONS

Seam allowances are ¼" (6 mm) unless otherwise noted.

Crochet the Layered Flower

1. Crochet a layered flower following the instructions and stitching diagram below. Leave at least 12" (30.5 cm) tail of yarn at the beginning of the first round; this will be used to attach the covered button in the center of the flower.

Gauge: *Size of crocheted layered flower is approximately 3" (7.6 cm) in diameter*

Start with adjustable ring.

Row 1: Ch 6 (counts as dc, ch 3), (dc, ch 3) 5 times in ring, join with a sl st in 3rd ch of beginning ch. (6 ch-3 spaces)

Rnd 2: Ch 1, (sc, hdc, 2 dc, hdc, sc) in each ch-3 space around, join with a sl st in first sc. (6 petals)

Rnd 3: Ch 1, working behind petals in Rnd 2, BPsc around the post of first dc in Rnd 1, ch 5, *BPsc around the post of next dc in Rnd 1, ch 5; rep from * around, join with a sl st in first sc. (6 ch-5 spaces)

Rnd 4: Ch 1, (sc, hdc, 3 dc, hdc, sc) in each ch-5 space around, join with a sl st in first sc. (6 petals)

Rnd 5: Ch 1, working behind petals in Rnd 2, BPsc around the post of first dc in Rnd 1, ch 6, *BPsc around the post of next dc in Rnd 1, ch 6; rep from * around, join with a sl st in first sc. (6 ch-6 spaces)

Rnd 6: Ch 1, (sc, hdc, 5 dc, hdc, sc) in each ch-6 space around, join with a sl st in first sc. (6 petals)
Fasten off.

Stitch Key

- ⊖ = chain
- • = slip stitch
- + = single crochet
- T = half double crochet
- ꓕ = double crochet
- ꝑ = back post single crochet
- ◎ = adjustable ring

Stitching Diagram

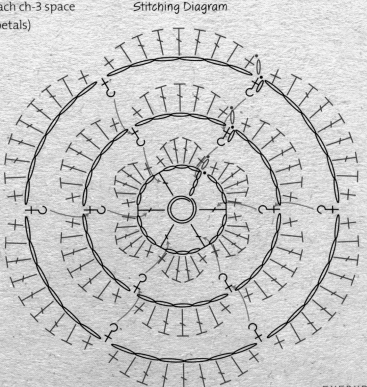

Assemble the Bag Charm

1. Cut the trims into various lengths, between 13" and 14" (33 and 35.6 cm) long. Fold all trims, except for the leather strip, in half widthwise. Using double strands of thread, stitch the trims together approximately 1/4" (6 mm) below the fold. Wrap the trims tightly together a few times and take several more stitches to attach the folded edges of the trim to the center back side of the flower. Be careful, as you are working with several layers of material. Pull the thread tight, make a knot, and cut off the excess thread.

Create and Attach Covered Button

1. Following the manufacturer's instructions, cover the fabric button with a coordinating cotton print scrap.

2. Thread the beginning yarn tail of the crocheted flower onto the tapestry needle and pass the needle through the back center to the front of the flower. Pass the yarn through the button shank and stitch to the center front of the flower several times. Wrap the shank with the yarn a few times and bring the needle to the back of the flower. Pull the yarn tightly, make a knot, and weave in the ends. Cut off the excess yarn tail.

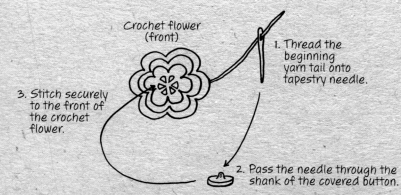

Crochet flower (front)

1. Thread the beginning yarn tail onto tapestry needle.

3. Stitch securely to the front of the crochet flower.

2. Pass the needle through the shank of the covered button.

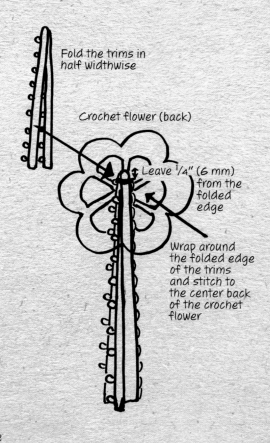

Fold the trims in half widthwise

Crochet flower (back)

Leave 1/4" (6 mm) from the folded edge

Wrap around the folded edge of the trims and stitch to the center back of the crochet flower

2. Fold the leather strip in half widthwise, as you did with the other trims. Using double strands of thread in matching color, wrap around the folded leather strip and attach to the center back side of the crochet flower, on top of the other trims. Repeat to wrap around the entire trims and stitch to the back side of the crochet flower, approximately ¾" (1.9 cm) below the first one.

3. Using two jewelry pliers, attach one 10 mm or larger sized jump ring to the upper center spoke of the crochet petal. Attach the 4" (10.2 cm) metal brass chain to the jump ring. At the opposite end of the metal chain, attach the clasp.

Tip

Stitch the leather strip to the back side of the crochet flower after the other trims are attached. The leather strip is thicker and trickier to work with, so it is best to stitch it separately from other trims.

Wrap around and stitch the trims to the back side of the crochet flower twice to secure the embellishment in place.

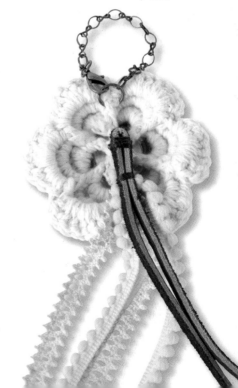

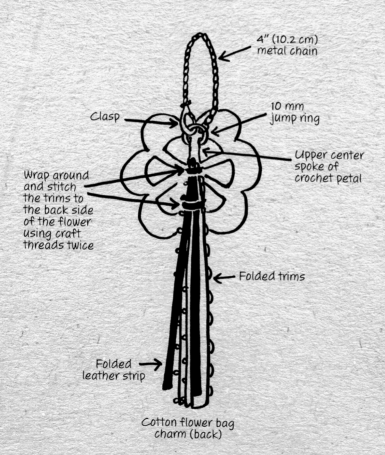

4" (10.2 cm) metal chain

Clasp

10 mm jump ring

Upper center spoke of crochet petal

Wrap around and stitch the trims to the back side of the flower using craft threads twice

Folded trims

Folded leather strip

Cotton flower bag charm (back)

BAGS AND POUCHES ZAKKA STYLE

I have made countless numbers of handmade bags and pouches over the years, and I have never grown tired of making them. By combining various fabrics, appliqué motifs, handmade tags, and crocheted or knitted parts, the possibilities of the bag and pouch design become endless! So be creative and add your personal touch to your own zakka style bags and pouches.

KOTORI ZIPPER POUCH

Finished Size: *5" × 4¼" (12.7 × 10.8 cm), not including the beak*

Kotori means little bird in Japanese. For this small zipper pouch, the wings are created with pieced scraps and the eyes are made with buttons. Carry around this bird in your purse and it will make you smile throughout the day. After making one, you may not be able to stop yourself from making a whole flock of birds! When you are preparing the exterior pouch, remember to reverse the wing and eye position for the back side of the bird so both sides of the bird's head face in the same direction.

MATERIALS

Fabric:

- linen piece, 12" × 6" (30.5 × 15.2 cm), for bird body
- cotton print, 12" × 6 (30.5 × 15.2m), for lining
- 5" (12.7 cm) square of yellow base cotton print, for beak
- six scrap pieces of assorted cotton print, at least 2" × 3" (5.1 × x 7.6 cm) each, for piecing bird wing

Other Supplies:

- batting, 12" × 6" (30.5 × 15.2 cm)
- lightweight paper-backed fusible web, at least 12" × 4" (30.5 × 10.2 cm), for attaching wings (I used HeatnBond Lite)
- 5" (12.7 cm) square fusible interfacing, for beak
- two buttons, for eyes
- strong thread, to securely sew the button to the pouch
- 5" (12.7 cm) zipper
- zipper foot of your sewing machine
- water-soluble pen
- basting spray, optional
- black or dark colored machine-sewing thread

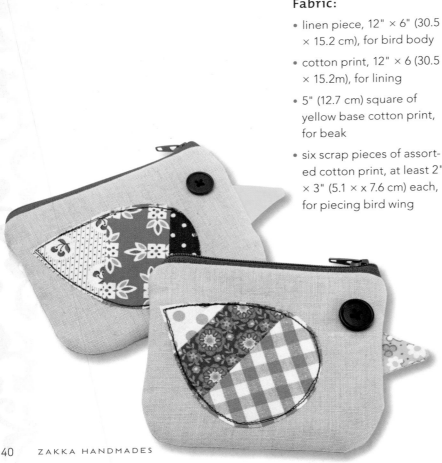

CUTTING INSTRUCTIONS

Trace the bird body, wing, and beak pattern pieces from page 123 onto tracing paper and cut out to make templates. Transfer the eye, wing, and beak lines marked for the bird body. Cut out a wing from the bird body template to make an open space in the center of the bird, based on the pattern. Mark "Front" and "Back" on each side of the bird body template. This will help you ensure that the head faces in the same direction on both sides of the bird.

Tip

Create a firm template of the bird body, wing, and beak pattern by transferring the pattern from the tracing paper created in step 1 to cardboard, such as from a cereal box. Then precisely mark the eye, wing, and beak lines to the linen piece and cut out the wing from the patched piece, which will follow in the next steps.

Prepare and Cut the Fabric

1. Using the template, cut out two body shapes each from the linen piece, lining fabric, and batting.

2. Fuse the interfacing on the wrong side of a 5" (12.7 cm) square of yellow cotton. Use the beak template to cut out two beaks.

INSTRUCTIONS

Seam allowances are ¼" (6 mm) unless otherwise noted.

Prepare the Bird Body

1. Spray-baste or pin the batting onto the wrong side of the linen body.

2. Using the bird body template as a guide, mark the eye, wing, and beak lines on the linen body using a water-soluble pen for the bird's *front*. Flip the body template to reverse, and repeat to make marks on the other linen body for the bird's *back*. This will ensure that the bird face of each pair faces the same direction.

Bird "front"

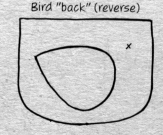
Bird "back" (reverse)

Flip the bird body template to reverse to make bird back

Select coordinating bright-colored prints for the pouch lining.

Prepare the Bird Body (cont.)

3. With right sides together, pin and sew two long sides of the yellow cotton beak pieces together, leaving the shortest side unsewn. See diagram.

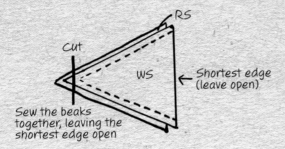

Cut

RS

WS

Shortest edge
(leave open)

Sew the beaks together, leaving the shortest edge open

4. Clip the pointed tip and excess seam of the beak. Turn the beak right side out and push out the tip of the beak with chopstick. Press.

5. Using the template as a guide, pin the beak to the bird front with the pointed tip of the beak facing inside of the body. Machine-stitch close to the edge using approximately ⅛" (3 mm) seam allowances; stitch several times to secure the beak to the body.

6. Using strong threads, sew the buttons to both sides of the linen body to create eyes. Follow the marked eye position to attach eyes.

Appliqué the Wings

1. Sew the fabric scraps together, creating two 4" × 3" (10.2 × 7.6 cm) rectangles.

2. Following the manufacturer's instructions, iron the fusible web onto the *wrong* sides of the pieced rectangles.

3. Trace the wing template onto the paper side of the pieced rectangle with a pencil. Cut out the wing. Repeat to make the second wing.

4. Peel off the paper backing and place the wing on the bird front, based on the marked wing line. Repeat to place another wing on the bird back. Press the wings in place.

5. Using black or dark-colored thread, topstitch twice around the wings close to the edge. Try to avoid the first stitching line when sewing around the second stitches, to add a hand-made look of irregular stitches.

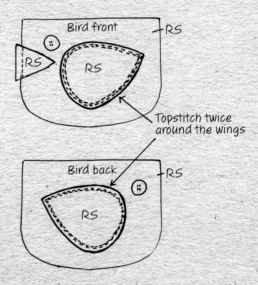

Bird front

RS

RS

RS

Topstitch twice around the wings

Bird back

RS

RS

Sew the Zipper

1. Change the sewing machine foot to the zipper foot. With right sides together, pin the zipper to the top edge of the bird front piece, as shown in the diagram. Open the zipper all the way down, and stitch the zipper to the bird front, close to the top edge. Once you've stitched

more than halfway, stop and lift the zipper foot, and zip the zipper shut so the zipper pull is out of the way. Lower the zipper foot again and continue sewing to complete the top edge.

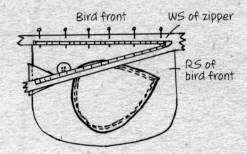

Bird front   WS of zipper

RS of bird front

2. Repeat to join the bird back piece to the zipper, with the remaining side of the zipper and the bird back piece facing right sides together. The diagram shows how the zipper is attached to both sides of the bird body.

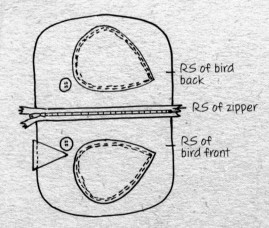

RS of bird back

RS of zipper

RS of bird front

3. With wrong side up, align the top edge of the lining piece along the wrong side of the zipper, so the zipper is sandwiched between the front exterior piece and the lining. Pin and stitch close to the zipper teeth, just *left* of the previous seam, to hide this seam. Repeat to sew the

other side of the zipper to the remaining lining piece. Now all four pieces—the bird exterior front, bird exterior back, and the two lining pieces—are sewn to the zipper.

4. Press fabrics in place from both sides.

Finish the Pouch

1. Change the machine foot back to the regular sewing foot. Bring both pieces of the bird exterior fabrics to one side and both pieces of the lining to the other side. With right sides together, pin around the entire pieces. Ensure that the teeth of both zipper ends are facing the *exterior* fabric. Unzip the zipper more than halfway. Start sewing from the bottom of the lining and stitch around all sides, leaving a 3" (7.6 cm) opening at the lining bottom.

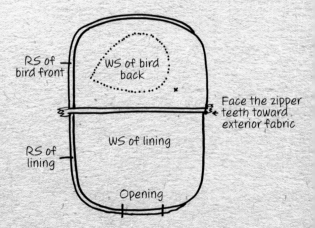

RS of bird front

WS of bird back

RS of lining

WS of lining

Face the zipper teeth toward exterior fabric

Opening

2. Using scissors, cut notches around the curves, taking care not to cut the seam. Turn the pouch right side out through the opening in the lining, and use a chopstick to push out the corners. Press. Hand-stitch or machine-stitch the opening closed.

For Variation

For a different look, I made this raindrop tote using a medium-weight linen for the exterior bag. Several different scraps of my favorite floral prints are used for the raindrops. The lining of this tote is a coordinating floral print, and the gingham check fabric is added for the straps.

RAINDROPS TOTE

Finished Size: *12½" × 12" × 2" (31.8 × 30.5 × 5.1 cm), without the straps*

Use this bag on a rainy day to lift the rainy day blues away! This tote bag also offers a great opportunity to use your pretty cotton print scraps and turn them into raindrop-shaped appliqué pieces. The backstitched embroidery is the falling rain. The tote is totally reversible so you can change the side of the bag on sunny days or anytime you want a different look.

MATERIALS

Fabric:

- ½ yd (0.46 m) or 44" × 18" (111.8 × 45.7 cm) medium-weight denim or navy linen, for exterior front and back panel
- ½ yd (0.46 m) or 44" × 18" (111.8 × 45.7 cm) navy with white polka dots print, for lining panels, lining sides, and inside pocket
- one fat eighth or 9" × 22" (22.9 × 55.9 cm) light blue and white gingham check print, for exterior sides
- one fat eighth or 9" × 22" (22.9 × 55.9 cm) red and white pin dots print, for straps
- ten scraps of assorted cotton print, each at least 3" × 4" (7.6 × 10.2 cm)

Other Supplies:

- ½ yd (0.46 m) of 45" (114.3 cm) width batting
- ¼ yd (0.23 m) of 17" (43.2 cm) width lightweight paper-backed fusible web (I used Heat'nBond Lite)
- 8" (20.3 cm) square heavy-weight fusible interfacing, for pocket
- embroidery floss or pearl cotton thread
- black or dark machine sewing thread
- pencil
- white marking pencil
- ruler
- basting spray, optional
- pins or sewing clips (I used Clover Wonder Clips)

Tsuyu, Japan's rainy season, runs every year in early summer. Humid, cloudy, rainy, and sometimes stormy weather lasts for several weeks throughout the islands of Japan. I designed this tote bag with Japan's tsuyu in mind, hoping that carrying a colorful raindrops tote like this one would keep the spirits positive even during the uncomfortable and inconvenient days of continued rain.

45

CUTTING INSTRUCTIONS

- Trace the rain drop and bag corner patterns on page 122 onto tracing paper, then onto a piece of firm cardboard, such as a cereal box, for easy cutting of appliqué pieces.
- Cut two 11" × 13" (27.9 × 33 cm) rectangles from medium-weight denim or navy linen, for exterior panels. Using bag corner template, mark the cutting line on both rectangles. Cut along the marked line.
- Cut two 11" × 13" (27.9 × 33 cm) rectangles from navy and white polka-dot print, for lining panels. Round the corners as for outer panels.
- Cut one 6" × 10" (15.2 × 25.4 cm) rectangle from navy and white polka-dot prints, for pocket.
- Cut two 2½" × 18" (6.4 × 45.7 cm) strips from light blue and white gingham check print, for exterior sides.
- Cut two 2½" × 18" (6.4 × 45.7 cm) strips from navy and white polka-dot print, for lining sides.
- Cut two 4" × 20" (10.2 × 50.8 cm) strips from red and white pin-dots print, for bag straps.
- Cut two 11" × 13" (27.9 × 33 cm) rectangles from batting, for front and back panels. Round the corners as for outer panels.
- Cut two 2½" × 18" strips (6.4 × 45.7 cm) from batting, for bag sides.
- Cut two 2" × 20" (5.1 × 51 cm) strips from batting, for bag straps.
- Cut one 6" × 5" (15.2 × 12.7 cm) rectangle from heavyweight fusible interfacing, for pocket.

INSTRUCTIONS

Seam allowances are ¼" (6 mm) unless otherwise noted.

Appliqué Raindrops

1. Following the manufacturer's instructions, iron the paper-backed fusible web onto the *wrong* side of the fabric scraps.

2. Using the template, trace 10 raindrops onto the paper side of the fusible web with a pencil. Cut out the pieces.

3. Peel off the paper backing and arrange five raindrops on the navy denim or linen exterior front panel, as shown in the diagram. Make sure the raindrops are at least 1" (2.5 cm) from all four edges of the panel. Ensure that all rainfall lines will run straight down from the top edge of the panel to the pointed tip of each raindrop, without touching other raindrops. Press and fuse the appliqué raindrops in place.

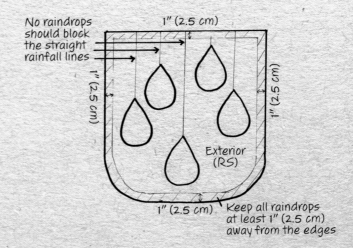

No raindrops should block the straight rainfall lines

1" (2.5 cm)

1" (2.5 cm)

1" (2.5 cm)

Exterior (RS)

1" (2.5 cm)

Keep all raindrops at least 1" (2.5 cm) away from the edges

4. Using black or dark thread, machine-stitch twice around each raindrop close to the edge.

5. Repeat the steps to add appliqué to the back panel of the exterior bag.

Embroider Falling Rain

1. Using a white marking pencil and a ruler, draw five straight lines from the top edge of the exterior front panel to the pointed tip of the raindrops.

2. Using backstitch, embroider the falling rain based on the marked lines.

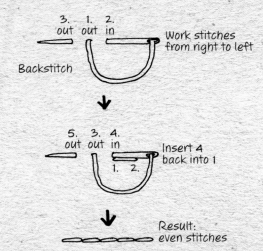

3. Repeat the steps to add embroidered falling rain to the back panel of the exterior bag.

Assemble the Exterior Bag

1. Spray-baste or pin the batting to the wrong sides of both the front and back panels of the exterior bag panels. Trim excess batting.

2. Spray-baste or pin the batting to the wrong side of two 2½" × 18" (6.4 × 45.7 cm) light blue and white gingham check strips. With right

sides facing, sew the short edges of the strips together to make one long bag side/bottom strip. Open seams and press. Trim any excess batting. Now you have a bag side/bottom strip that is 2½" × 35½" (6.4 × 90.2 cm) long.

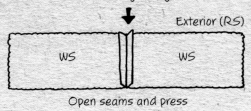

3. Mark the center on the right side of the exterior front panel along the bottom edge. With right sides together, pin the exterior front panel to the bag side/bottom strip, aligning the marked center of the front panel's bottom edge and the opened seam line of the side/bottom strip, as shown in the diagram. Cut off any excess strip ends at the top edge. Sew the pieces together. Using scissors, cut notches around the curves, taking care not to cut the seam. Press to open the seams.

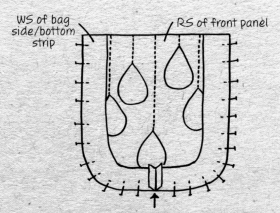

Align marked center of bottom of front panel and the open seam line of bag side/bottom strip

Assemble the Exterior Bag (cont.)

4. Repeat step 3 to join the exterior back panel to the remaining bag side/bottom strip. Using scissors, cut notches around the curves, taking care not to cut the seam. Press to open seams.

Make and Add Straps

1. Fold the 4" × 20" (10.2 × 50.8 cm) red and white pin-dot strip in half lengthwise, wrong sides together. Press and unfold. Fold the long edges to meet in the center; then press again. Open the strip and place a 2" × 20" (5.1 × 50.8 cm) piece of batting in the center of the wrong side of the strip. Fold the long edge of the rectangle over the batting, hiding the raw edges. Refold again and press. Pin or use sewing clips to hold the strap together. Topstitch along both long edges. Repeat to make the remaining strap. You now have two straps that are approximately 1" × 20" (2.5 × 50.8 cm) long.

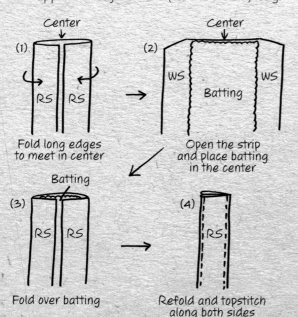

(1) Center
Fold long edges to meet in center
RS RS

(2) Center
WS Batting WS
Open the strip and place batting in the center

(3) Batting
RS RS
Fold over batting

(4) RS
Refold and topstitch along both sides

2. Pin both ends of one bag strap to the top edge of the right side of the bag front, aligning the raw edges, as illustrated. Make sure the strap is centered with 4" (10.2 cm) between the ends. Machine-baste the strap ends 1/8" (3 mm) from the top edge. Repeat with second strap and bag back.

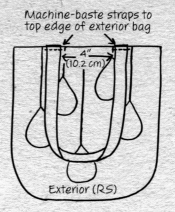

Machine-baste straps to top edge of exterior bag

4" (10.2 cm)

Exterior (RS)

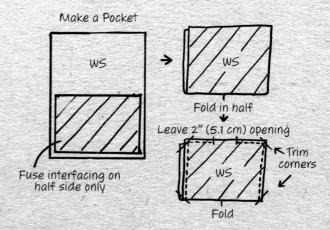

Make a Pocket

WS → WS

Fold in half

Fuse interfacing on half side only

Leave 2" (5.1 cm) opening

Trim corners

WS

Fold

Assemble Pockets and Bag Lining

1. Fold the 6" × 10" (15.2 × 25.4 cm) navy and white polka-dot print rectangle in half widthwise, right sides together, to form a 6" × 5" (15.2 × 12.7 cm) rectangle. Open the rectangle and fuse the 6" × 5" (15.2 × 12.7 cm) piece of fusible interfacing to the wrong side, to only half of the rectangle. Fold the pocket in half, right sides together, and pin. Sew along three open edges, leaving a 2" (5.1 cm) opening along the edge opposite the fold. Trim all corners and press seams open.

2. Turn the pocket right side out through the opening and press flat. Topstitch twice along the folded edge, approximately ⅛" (3 mm) and ¼" (6 mm) from the folded edge.

3. Center the pocket on the right side of the lining panel, 2" (5.1 cm) from the top. Pin the pocket in place. Stitch around both sides and the bottom of the pocket, ⅛" (3 mm) from the edge, leaving the top edge open. Backstitch at the beginning and end to reinforce and secure the pocket.

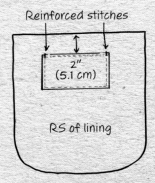

Reinforced stitches

2" (5.1 cm)

RS of lining

4. Just as you made the bag side/bottom strip for the exterior bag, make one long side/bottom strip for the bag lining. With right sides together, sew the short edges of the 2½" × 18" (6.4 × 45.7 cm) navy and white polka-dot strips together. Open the seams and press. Now you have a side/bottom strip for the bag lining that is 2½" × 35½" (6.4 × 90.2 cm).

5. Repeat Assemble the Exterior Bag steps 3 and 4, using lining panels and lining strip, to assemble the bag lining. However, this time leave a 5" (12.7 cm) opening on one side of the bag lining for turning the bag right side out.

Finish the Tote

1. With right sides together, insert the exterior bag inside the bag lining. Straps should be sandwiched between the exterior bag and the lining. Match side seams, and align and pin the raw edges at the top. Sew around the upper edges of the bag, backstitching over straps for reinforcement.

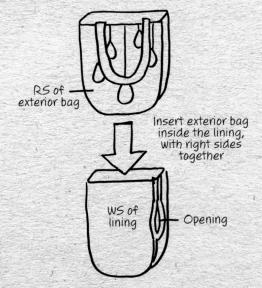

RS of exterior bag

Insert exterior bag inside the lining, with right sides together

WS of lining

Opening

2. Turn the bag and lining right side out through the opening in the lining. Hand- or machine-stitch to close the opening.

3. Push the lining inside the exterior bag and press. Topstitch ⅛" (3 mm) from the upper edge to finish the tote.

ROLL-UP ECO SHOPPER BAG

Finished Size: *19" × 21" (48.3 × 53.3 cm), including the handles*

This is an eco-friendly, oversized, and fully reversible shopping bag that can be rolled up nicely into a compact size. It is sewn without any interfacing, so the bag rolls up small enough to carry with you in your purse at all times. Bring this bag shopping or to the gym or library, when traveling, or otherwise as your everyday bag. When cutting the fabrics, cut pieces for two coordinating bags at once—Roll-Up Eco Shopper Bag and Mini Drawstring Pouch (page 56)—by referring to the cutting layout shown below. The matching Mini Drawstring Pouch can be made from the cutout remnants of this bag's inner handles.

MATERIALS

Fabric:

- ¾ yd (0.69 m) or 44" × 27" (111.8 × 68.6 cm) floral cotton print, for the exterior bag
- ¾ yd (0.69 m) or 44" × 27" (111.8 × 68.6 cm) polka-dot cotton print, for the lining and tie ribbons

CUTTING INSTRUCTIONS

- Refer to the bag pattern on page 125 to make a bag template.
- Optional: Make a matching Mini Drawstring Pouch on page 56 using the cutout remnants from this bag's inner handles. Follow the cutting layout to the right.

- Cut all fabrics based on the cutting layout to the right.
- Double fold the fabric and cut out two bag pieces from the floral cotton print, using the bag pattern.
- Double fold the fabric and cut out two bag pieces from the polka-dot cotton print, using the bag pattern.
- Cut two 14" × 1½" (35.6 × 3.8 cm) strips from the polka-dot cotton print, for tie ribbons.

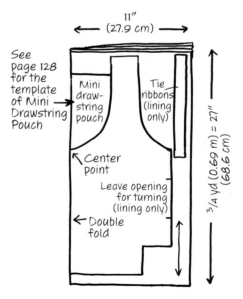

Cutting Layout of Exterior and Lining Fabrics

INSTRUCTIONS

Seam allowances are ¼" (6 mm) unless otherwise noted.

Sew Both Sides of the Bag

1. Sew the exterior bag. With right sides facing, pin the front and back pieces of the exterior bag together. Sew both sides and the bottom edges together, as shown in the diagram. Press all seams open.

Tip

Placing a roll-up towel inside the bag will make it easier to press open the seams.

2. Create a box-shaped bottom for the exterior bag. With right sides together, match the bottom seam line to the side seam line of one side of the exterior bag. Pin along the edge and sew the seams together. Repeat for the remaining open side. Now you've sewn the exterior bag. Repeat to sew the bag lining together, but for the lining, leave a 4" (10.2 cm) opening on one side of the bag for turning.

Assemble the Tie Ribbons

1. Refer to the diagram. Fold down ¼" (6 mm) inward on one short edge of the 14" × 1½" (35.6 × 3.8 cm) strip and press. Then fold the strip in half lengthwise, wrong sides together. Press and unfold. Fold the long edges to meet in the center, and press again. Topstitch along three edges. Repeat to make the remaining tie. Now you have two tie ribbons.

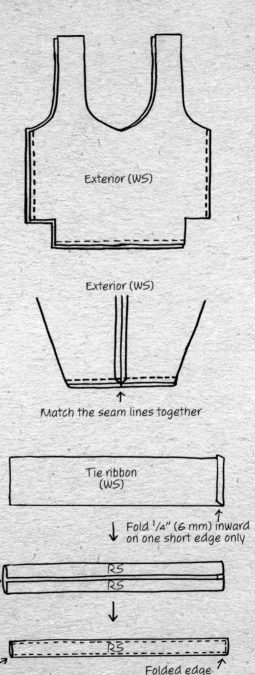

Exterior (WS)

Exterior (WS)

Match the seam lines together

Tie ribbon (WS)

Fold ¼" (6 mm) inward on one short edge only

Center →

RS
RS

RS

Raw edge →

Folded edge

2. Align and pin the raw edge of one tie to the center point of the exterior bag's right side. Sew the tie close to the opening top edge of the exterior bag, using 1/8" (3 mm) seam allowances, going back and forth to secure. Repeat on the other side of the exterior bag.

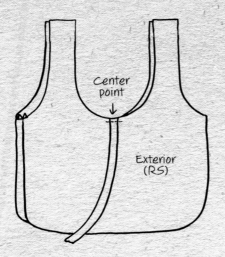

Center point

Exterior (RS)

Tip

Frequent ironing is the key to creating a clean finish. Keep your iron handy to make a neat-looking bag.

Sew the Exterior Bag and Lining Together

1. With right sides together, insert the lining inside the exterior bag. Pin the exterior bag and the lining together along the inner and outer handles of the bag opening. Make sure the tie ribbons on the front and back sides of the bag are sandwiched between the exterior bag and the lining. Sew the inner handles together, leaving 4" (10.2 cm) unsewn on both ends of the inner handles, as illustrated. Backstitch over the tie ribbons for reinforcement. Repeat on the other side of the bag.

Tip

Using a handmade ironing template will make it easier to press long, narrow rectangles in half lengthwise to create tie ribbons. Cut out a 12" × 2" (30.5 × 5.1 cm) rectangle from a piece of cardboard, such as a cereal box. Use it as an ironing template by placing it underneath the folded edges of the fabric strip and press.

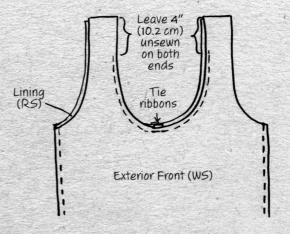

Leave 4" (10.2 cm) unsewn on both ends

Lining (RS)

Tie ribbons

Exterior Front (WS)

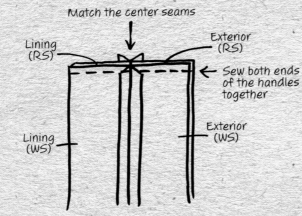

Bag side

Sew the bag handles together

Match side seams together

Lining (RS)

Exterior side (WS)

Match the center seams

Lining (RS)

Exterior (RS)

Sew both ends of the handles together

Lining (WS)

Exterior (WS)

Lining (WS)

Exterior (WS)

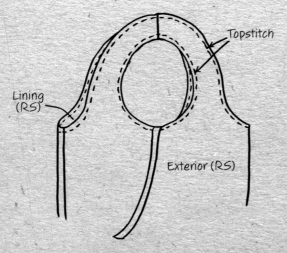

Topstitch

Lining (RS)

Exterior (RS)

Sew the Exterior Bag and Lining Together (cont.)

2. Now sew the outer handles together. Position the bag to the bag side and align the side seams. Referring to the diagram, pin and sew the exterior and lining handles together in a U shape, from one top edge of the handle to another. Repeat for the other side of the bag. Open and press all seams of the inner and outer handles. Carefully cut notches around the curves.

3. Turn the bag right side out through the opening in the lining. Bring the two handles together from the *front* side of the bag to create a loop by twisting both ends. With right sides together, match the center seams of both raw edges of the handles. Pin and sew both ends of the handle together. Repeat for the back side of the bag to create another handle. Press to open both seams of connected handles.

4. Press around the entire handles. Topstitch around the inner and outer edge of the handles, ⅛" (3 mm) from the edge, catching the unsewn opening of the inner handles. Hand-stitch or machine-stitch the side opening of the lining closed.

HOW TO FOLD THE ROLL-UP
ECO SHOPPER BAG IN COMPACT

1. First fold the handles and the bottom inward.

2. Fold both sides three- to four-fold.

3. Roll up the bag from the bottom up.

4. Wrap around the tie ribbons and tuck the ribbon ends underneath.

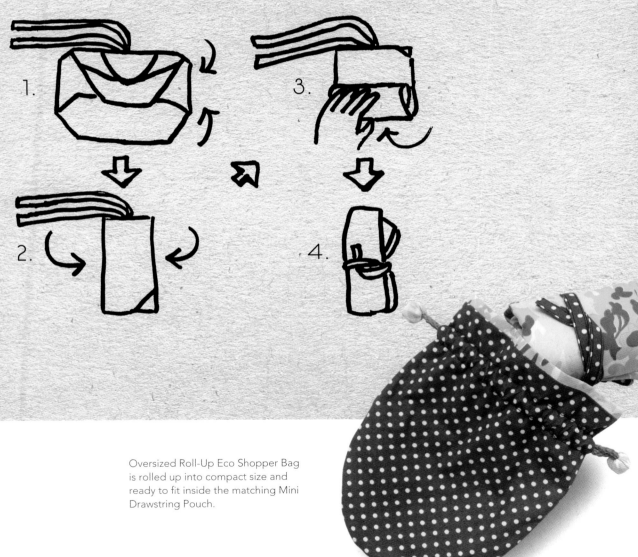

Oversized Roll-Up Eco Shopper Bag is rolled up into compact size and ready to fit inside the matching Mini Drawstring Pouch.

MINI DRAWSTRING POUCH

Finished Size: *7½" × 8¾" (19.1 × 22.2 cm)*

This Mini Drawstring Pouch forms into a pretty oval shape when the drawstrings are pulled at the opening. Simply cut out fabric pieces using the pattern on page 128, or use cutout remnants from the Roll-Up Eco Shopper Bag on page 50 to make a matching bag set. For this drawstring pouch, I embellished the linen bag with pretty lace and alphabet ribbon trim to create a romantic style pouch. For other options, stitch embroidery, apply appliqué, or sew a crocheted doily piece onto the linen bag. The size of this pouch is ideal to store your cell phone, small gadgets, accessories, cosmetics, or various cards, or to carry the folded Rolled-Up Eco Shopper Bag snugly inside.

MATERIALS

Fabric:

- one fat eighth or 22" × 9" (55.9 × 22.9 cm) medium-weight linen, for the exterior bag
- one fat eighth or 22" × 9" (55.9 × 22.9 cm) striped cotton, for the lining

Other Supplies:

- lace, ribbon trims, and other embellishments, to decorate the exterior panels, optional
- water-soluble pen
- ruler
- chopstick or tapered awl
- two 19" (48.3 cm) cotton or acrylic cords
- large safety pin or bodkin, to thread cords through the pouch opening
- cotton balls, to wipe off the marked lines of water-soluble pen

CUTTING INSTRUCTIONS

- Refer to the pattern on page 128 and make a template for the pouch. Be sure to transfer the two drawstring opening lines on the exterior bag and one opening for turning on the lining.

- Using the template, cut out two each from the exterior and lining fabrics (total of four pieces). Or, use four remnant cutout pieces from cutting the inner handles of the Roll-Up Eco Shopper Bag (page 51).

Drawstring bags are called *kinchaku* in Japanese. The *kinchaku* style bag has been used in Japan over the centuries, valued for its simple yet functional uses. In the early days *kinchaku* bags were used to store money, the family seal, good luck charms, and other precious items.

INSTRUCTIONS

Seam allowances are ¼" (6 mm) unless otherwise noted.

Embellish the Exterior Bag

1. Optional embellishment: Using lace, trim ribbons, and other embellishments, decorate both sides of the exterior panels as desired.

Assemble the Pouch

1. With right sides facing, pin the exterior panel and the lining panel together at the top edge. Sew along the top edge. Open seams and press. Repeat with the remaining exterior panel and the lining panel.

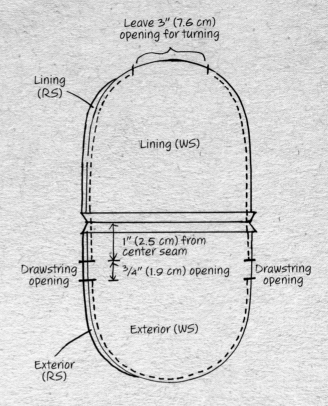

Leave 3" (7.6 cm) opening for turning

Lining (RS)

Lining (WS)

1" (2.5 cm) from center seam

¾" (1.9 cm) opening

Drawstring opening

Drawstring opening

Exterior (WS)

Exterior (RS)

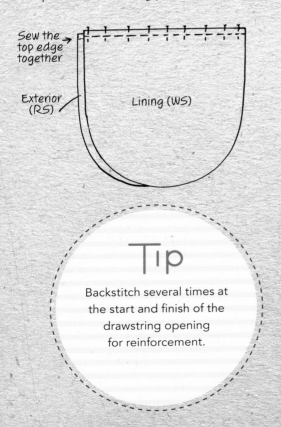

Sew the top edge together

Exterior (RS)

Lining (WS)

Tip

Backstitch several times at the start and finish of the drawstring opening for reinforcement.

2. With right sides facing, bring both pieces of the lining and both pieces of the exterior to the same side, as illustrated. Pin and sew around the pieces, leaving ¾" (1.9 cm) drawstring opening on both sides of the exterior bag and a 3" (7.6 cm) opening for turning on the lining.

3. Open the seams and press around the entire edge. Using a pair of scissors, cut notches around the curves, taking care not to cut the seam. Turn the pouch right side out through the 3" (7.6 cm) opening in the lining and use a chopstick to push out the corners. Press. Hand-stitch or machine-stitch the opening closed.

4. Insert the lining inside the exterior bag. Position the top edge of the lining so it shows approximately ¼" (6 mm) above the top edge of the exterior bag, as shown in the diagram. Press the pouch opening in place.

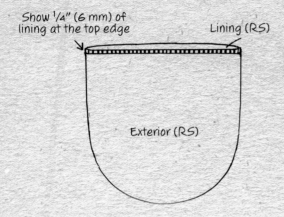

Show ¼" (6 mm) of lining at the top edge

Lining (RS)

Exterior (RS)

Pass Cords through the Bag

1. Using a water-soluble pen and a ruler, draw two lines below the top edge of the exterior bag, as illustrated. The first line is drawn 1¼" (3.2 cm) below the top edge, and the second line is drawn ¾" (1.9 cm) below the first line. These lines should match up with the drawstring openings that are left unsewn at step 2 of Assemble the Pouch. Connect the lines on both sides to stretch all the way around the pouch.

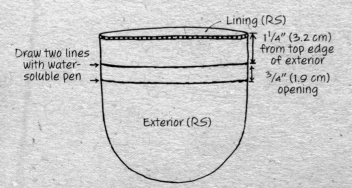

Draw two lines with water-soluble pen →

Lining (RS)

1¼" (3.2 cm) from top edge of exterior

¾" (1.9 cm) opening

Exterior (RS)

Tip

Insert the tip of a chopstick or tapered awl from the exterior bag's drawstring opening to push the seam inward. This will help pass the cords easily at a later step.

2. Topstitch two lines around the right side of the exterior bag based on the marked lines. The lining is sewn together with the exterior bag. You now have two stitched lines at the top of the pouch. Wet the cotton ball and wipe off the marked lines of water-soluble pen from the exterior bag.

3. Using a large safety pin or bodkin, thread one 19" (48.3 cm) cord through an opening and pass the cord all the way around and return to where you started. Tie the knot ends securely together. Thread the remaining cord from another opening and repeat.

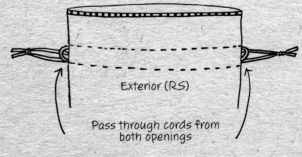

Exterior (RS)

Pass through cords from both openings

VINTAGE RIBBON FLEX FRAME POUCH

Finished Size: *4¾" × 8" (12.1 × 20.3 cm) with 4" (10.2 cm) width at the opening*

The flex frame pouch is unique and convenient to use. It opens with just one hand by simply squeezing the sides. For this pouch, a 4" (10.2 cm) flex frame is inserted through the casing. The pouch size is suitable for storing a pair of sunglasses, eyeglasses, pens and pencils, crochet hooks, scissors, and other craft items. You may shorten the pouch lengths to fit your smart phones and other gadgets. Besides decorating the pouch with vintage jacquard ribbons, embellish the pouch with other flourishes, such as vintage lace, doily, cotton tape, ricrac and pompom trims to make your original zakka style flex frame pouch.

MATERIALS

Fabric:

- one fat eighth or 22" × 9" (55.9 × 22.9 cm) medium-weight linen, for exterior
- one fat eighth or 22" × 9" (55.9 × 22.9 cm) coordinating solid cotton, for lining
- scrap of coordinating cotton print, at least 11" × 5" (27.9 × 12.7 cm), for the casing

Other Supplies:

- 12" × 9" (30.5 × 22.9 cm) batting
- jacquard ribbon, lace, trims, crocheted doily, or other embellishments, to decorate the linen exterior (For this pouch, I used 16" [40.6 cm] of 2" [5.1 cm] jacquard ribbon on the front and back sides of the pouch.)
- 1½" (3.8 cm) of ½" (1.3 cm) width ribbon trim, for side tab embellishment, optional
- flex frame, 4" (10.2 cm) width
- basting spray, optional
- pliers, to close the screw pin of the flex frame
- sewing clips, optional (I used Clover Wonder Clips.)

CUTTING INSTRUCTIONS

- Cut two 5½" × 8" (14 × 20.3 cm) rectangles from the linen, for exterior.
- Cut two 5¼" × 8" (13.5 × 20.3 cm) rectangles from coordinating solid cotton, for lining.
- Cut four 5" × 2¼" (12.7 × 5.7 cm) rectangles from coordinating cotton print, for casing.
- Cut two 5½" × 8" (14 × 20.3 cm) rectangles from batting.

Tip

The width of lining panels is intentionally sized slightly narrower than the exterior panels by ¼" (6 mm) so the lining will fit smoothly inside the exterior pouch.

INSTRUCTIONS

Seam allowances are ¼" (6 mm) unless otherwise noted.

Embellish the Exterior Panels

1. Spray-baste or pin the batting onto the wrong sides of two exterior linen panels.

2. Using jacquard ribbon, lace, trims, crocheted doily, or other embellishments, decorate the linen panels as desired.

Assemble the Casing

1. Refer to the diagram to create two casings. Layer two 5" × 2¼" (12.7 × 5.7 cm) rectangles together with right sides facing. Pin and sew the short edges together, leaving the long edges unsewn. Turn right side out and press. Fold the rectangle in half lengthwise. Repeat with the remaining two 5" × 2¼" (12.7 × 5.7 cm) rectangles to create a second casing.

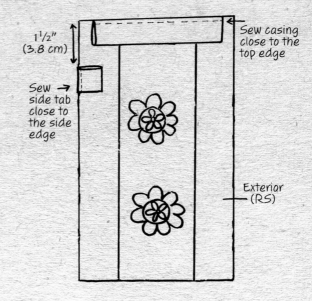

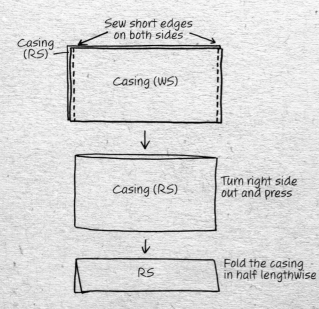

Assemble the Exterior

1. Sew the casing to the exterior panels. Aligning the raw edges, center the casing on the top edge of the exterior panel's right side. The folded side of the casing is placed inside of the exterior panel. Pin and sew close to the top edge. Repeat for the remaining exterior panel to attach the casing.

2. Optional side tab embellishment: Sew the side tab to the exterior panel. Fold 1½" (3.8 cm) of ½" (1.3 cm) width ribbon trim in half widthwise, wrong sides together. Aligning the raw edges, pin the ends of the ribbon trims to the side edge of the exterior linen panel, 1½" (3.8 cm) from the top edge. Sew closely along the edge.

3. With right sides facing, pin the assembled front and back exterior linen panels together, leaving the top open. Referring to the diagram, flip the casings *upward*, keeping them outside of the exterior pouch. Sew two exterior panels together, being careful not to catch the casings. Press with the tip of the iron to open seams around all three edges. Trim the bottom corners.

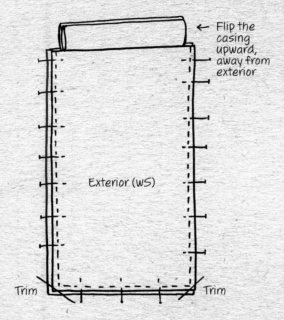

Flip the casing upward, away from exterior

Exterior (WS)

Trim   Trim

Assemble the Lining

1. With right sides facing, pin and sew three sides of the lining together, leaving a 3" (7.6 cm) opening in one side for turning. Open the seams and press. Trim the bottom corners. Turn the lining right side out through the top opening. Use a chopstick to push out the corners.

Finish the Flex Frame Pouch

1. With right sides together, insert the lining inside the exterior pouch. Flip the casings *down* inside the exterior pouch, so that the casings are sandwiched between the lining and the exterior. Match the side seams, align, and pin the raw edges at the top. Pin or clip all three pieces together (exterior, casing, and lining) at the opening. Sew around the upper edges of the pouch.

2. Turn the pouch right side out through the opening in the lining. Use a chopstick to push out the corners. Hand-stitch or machine-stitch to close the opening of the lining. Press both casings upward, away from the exterior pouch.

3. Carefully slide the flex frame from one side of the pouch and pass through both casings. Following the manufacturer's instruction, insert the screw pin in place using a pliers to close the flex frame.

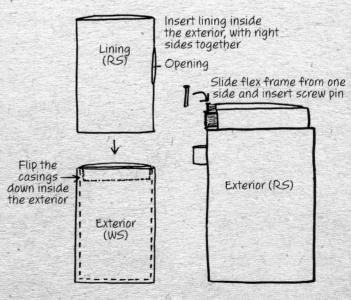

Lining (RS)

Insert lining inside the exterior, with right sides together

Opening

Slide flex frame from one side and insert screw pin

Flip the casings down inside the exterior

Exterior (WS)

Exterior (RS)

CROCHET DOILY AND LINEN POUCH

Finished Size: *5¾" × 4" (14.6 × 10.2 cm)*

The body of this pouch is made of medium-weight linen and the pouch flap is made of a hand-crocheted doily. The doily is worked in rounds and finished with pretty scallops. When you crochet the final round of the doily, stop crocheting after making seven scallops and leave the remaining edge without scallops. Only the finished scallops will be visible and used as a flap, while the edges without the scallops will be hidden inside the lining. Make your own covered button with a coordinating fabric scrap and use the small gap of the doily's center scallop as a buttonhole.

MATERIALS

Fabric:

- one fat eighth or 22" × 9" (55.9 × 22.9 cm) medium-weight linen, for exterior
- one fat eighth or 22" × 9" (55.9 × 22.9 cm) cotton print, for lining
- small scrap of coordinating cotton print, at least 2" (5.1 cm) square, to make a covered button

Other Supplies:

- batting, 14" × 5" (35.6 × 12.7 cm), for the pouch
- 11 yd (10 m) 100% four-ply cotton yarn. Sample uses Lily Sugar 'n Cream in Ecru. (Yarn weight: 4 Medium)
- size 8/H (5.0 mm) crochet hook
- one size 36 (⅞" or 2.2 cm) covered button and kit
- basting spray, optional
- strong thread, to securely sew the button to the pouch
- water-soluble pen, optional
- fabric glue, optional
- steam iron

CUTTING INSTRUCTIONS

- Trace the pattern on page 126 to make template for the pouch.
- Using the pouch template, cut two panels each from the medium-weight linen, cotton print, and batting.

INSTRUCTIONS

Crochet the Doily

Gauge: *Size of crocheted doily is approximately 4¼" (10.8 cm) square*

1. Crochet a doily following the instruction and stitching diagram below. After stitching, pin the doily into shape on a flat ironing board. Hold steam iron above the crocheted piece and steam into shape.

Start with adjustable ring.

Rnd 1: Ch 4 (counts as dc, ch 1), (dc, ch 1) 11 times in ring, join with a sl st in 3rd ch of beginning ch. (12 ch-1 spaces)

Rnd 2: Sl st in next ch-1 space, ch 3 (counts as dc), dc in same ch-1 space, ch 1, *2 dc in next ch-1 space, ch 1; rep from * around, join with a sl st in top of beginning ch-3. (12 ch-1 spaces)

Rnd 3: Sl st in next ch-1 space, ch 3 (counts as dc), dc in same ch-1 space, ch 3, *2 dc in next ch-1 space, ch 3; rep from * around, join with a sl st in top of beginning ch-3. (12 ch-3 spaces)

Work now progresses in a row.

Row 4: Sl st in next dc, (sc, hdc, 3 dc, hdc, sc) in each of next 7 ch-3 space, sl st in next dc. (7 scallops) Fasten off.

Stitch Key

- ⌒ = chain
- • = slip stitch
- ✝ = single crochet
- ⊤ = half double crochet
- ⊤ = double crochet
- ◎ = adjustable ring

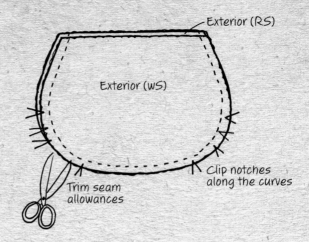

Exterior (RS)

Exterior (WS)

Trim seam allowances

Clip notches along the curves

Sew the Exterior

Seam allowances are ¼" (6 mm) unless otherwise noted.

1. Spray-baste or pin the batting to the wrong sides of the exterior linen panels. With right sides facing, pin and sew the front and back exterior linen panels together, leaving the top open. Carefully cut notches around the curves. Trim seam allowances to approximately ⅛" (3 mm) to minimize bulkiness.

Sew the Lining

1. Just as you sewed the exterior pouch, pin and sew the front and back lining panels together, with right sides facing and leaving the top open. Leave a 2½" (6.4 cm) opening for turning at the bottom edge of the lining panels. Carefully cut notches around the curves.

Stitching Diagram

Assemble the Pouch

1. With right sides facing, insert the lining inside the exterior pouch and match the side seams together. Then insert the crocheted doily between the exterior panel and the lining panel, with seven scalloped edges placed *inside* the pouch and the doily's round edges (without the scallops) placed *outside* the pouch from the top opening. The doily should face right side together with the linen exterior panel. Pin around the pouch opening and carefully sew the layers together using your sewing machine. Turn the pouch right side out from the opening of the lining.

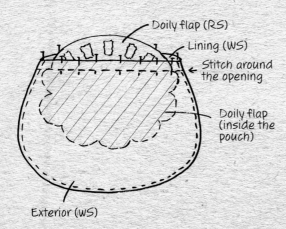

2. Following the manufacturer's instructions, cover the fabric button with a coordinating cotton print scrap. Refer to the tip on page 36 for how to add batting to the covered button.

3. Using a water-soluble pen, make a mark on the front right side of the exterior pouch, approximately 1¾" (4.5 cm) from the bottom edge, centered. Close the flap over the pouch to see if the marked button position matches with the center gap of the doily's scallop edging. If it doesn't, adjust your button position accordingly. Using strong thread, hand-stitch the covered button to the exterior pouch. Passing the threads through the opening of the lining may be helpful when stitching the button.

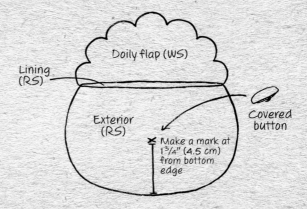

4. Hand-stitch or machine-stitch the opening of the lining closed. Press the exterior pouch and lining for a neat finish.

SIMPLE LINEN TOTE

Finished size of tote: *Approximately 11½" × 13½" (29.2 × 34.3 cm), not including the straps*
Length of straps: *Approximately 19" (48.3 cm)*

This is a flat shaped tote bag that is simple to sew. In general, I like to make my handmade bags reversible and this one is no exception, with medium-weight linen used on one side and cotton print on the reverse. Enjoy both sides of the tote according to your style. Fuse heavyweight interfacing to the tote straps and optional pocket. I skipped the batting or interfacing for the bag itself, but you may add them if you wish. Embellish the tote with the Cotton Flower Bag Charm on page 34.

MATERIALS

Fabric:

- ½ yd (0.46 m) or 44" × 18" (111.8 × 45.7 cm) medium-weight linen, for exterior
- ½ yd (0.46 m) or 44" × 18" (111.8 × 45.7 cm) gingham check print, for lining
- one fat quarter or 22" × 18" (55.9 × 45.7 cm) floral cotton print, for straps and pocket, optional

Other Supplies:

- ½ yd (0.46 m) heavyweight fusible interfacing

CUTTING INSTRUCTIONS

- Cut two 12" × 14" (30.5 cm × 35.6 cm) rectangles from medium-weight linen.
- Cut two 12" × 14" (30.5 × 35.6 cm) rectangles from gingham check print.
- Cut two 2½" × 20" (6.4 × 50.8 cm) strips from floral cotton print, for straps.
- Cut one 6" × 10" (15.2 cm × 25.4 cm) rectangle from floral cotton print, for pocket, optional.
- Cut two 2½" × 20" (6.4 × 50.8 cm) strips from heavyweight interfacing, for straps.
- Cut one 6" × 5" (15.2 × 12.7 cm) rectangle from heavyweight interfacing, for pocket, optional.

Enjoy the reversible side of tote too!

INSTRUCTIONS

Seam allowances are ¼" (6 mm) unless otherwise noted.

Assemble the Exterior Bag

1. With right sides facing, pin and sew three sides of the exterior panels together, leaving the top edge open. Open seams and press. Trim the bottom corners.

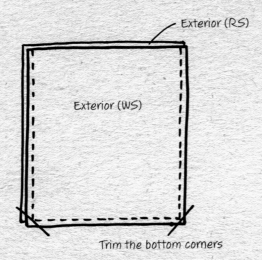

Exterior (RS)

Exterior (WS)

Trim the bottom corners

Make a Pocket (Optional)

1. Create a pocket using 6" × 10" (15.2 × 25.4 cm) floral print rectangle and 6" × 5" (15.2 × 12.7 cm) fusible interfacing, following instructions in steps 1-2 of Assemble Pockets and Bag Lining of the Raindrops Tote (page 48).

2. Center the pocket on the right side of the gingham check print rectangle, 2" (5.1 cm) from the top edge. Pin in place. Using ⅛" (3 mm) seam allowances, stitch around both sides and bottom of the pocket, leaving the top edge open. Repeat stitches several times at the beginning and end to reinforce and secure the pocket in place.

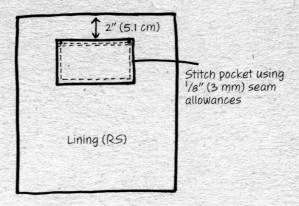

2" (5.1 cm)

Stitch pocket using ⅛" (3 mm) seam allowances

Lining (RS)

Assemble the Lining

1. Repeat step 1 of Assemble Exterior Bag to assemble the bag lining using two gingham check panels. However, this time leave a 5" (12.7 cm) opening on one side of the bag lining for turning the bag right side out.

Make and Add Straps

1. Fuse a 2½" × 20" (6.4 × 50.8 cm) strip of heavyweight interfacing to the entire wrong side of a 2½" × 20" (6.4 × 50.8 cm) strip, following manufacturer's instructions. Fold the long edges in half lengthwise, wrong sides together, and press. Then fold the long edges to meet in the center and press. Pin and topstitch

⅛" (3 mm) from both long edges. Repeat to make the remaining strap. You now have two straps that are approximately 20" × ¾" (50.8 × 1.9 cm) long.

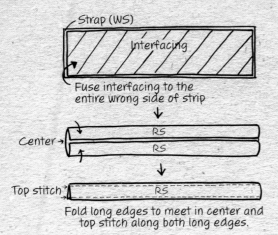

Strap (WS)

Interfacing

Fuse interfacing to the entire wrong side of strip

Center →

RS

RS

Top stitch

RS

Fold long edges to meet in center and top stitch along both long edges.

2. Pin both ends of the strap to the front top edge of the linen exterior bag, aligning the raw edges. Make sure the strap is centered with 4" (10.2 cm) between the ends. Machine-baste the strap ends ⅛" (3 mm) from the top edge. Repeat with the second strap and the remaining back side of the linen exterior bag.

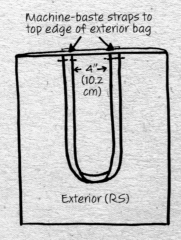

Machine-baste straps to top edge of exterior bag

← 4" →
(10.2 cm)

Exterior (RS)

Finish the Tote

1. With right sides together, insert the lining inside the exterior bag. The straps should be sandwiched between the exterior bag and the lining. Match the side seams together and align and pin the raw edges at the top. Sew around the upper edges of the tote, backstitching over straps for reinforcement.

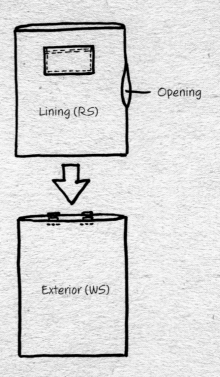

Opening

Lining (RS)

Exterior (WS)

2. Turn the bag right side out through the opening in the lining. Use a chopstick to push out the corners. Hand-stitch or machine-stitch to close the opening of the lining.

3. Topstitch ⅛" (3 mm) from the upper edge of the bag opening to finish the tote.

BABY AND YOUNG CHILD ZAKKA

Many of the children's zakka in this book were initially made for my own girls, including Children's Pencil Bag and Puffy Bow Ponytail. After several attempts, I designed these children's zakka to meet their fussy taste! After all, there is nothing more flattering to actually see young people wearing and using my handmade zakka. I love to see how the cute baby looks even cuter with my handmade bib and baby shoes on. It makes me very happy when I see our children's friends using my handmade bags and pouches. That's why I can never stop creating handmade zakka for children.

PATCHWORK BIB

Finished Size: *9" × 10" (22.9 × 25.4 cm) when side closure is closed*

I made this bib for my youngest nephew, Joe. He lives with his parents near the Ueno Zoo in Tokyo, Japan, where giant pandas are housed. I wrote Joe's name directly onto the bib's front linen panel using a water-soluble pen and then hand-embroidered his name with backstitches. For the reverse side of the bib, I used double gauze for its softness and absorbency (flannel or cotton terry is a good alternative). The side closure of the bib makes it easier for the mom and dad to put the bib on and off of the baby—even when the baby is sleeping.

MATERIALS

Fabric:

- 12" (30.5 cm) square cotton print, for the bib top
- 12" × 3" (30.5 cm × 7.6 cm) rectangle linen, for the bib center
- three pieces of assorted cotton scraps, each at least 4" (10.2 cm) square, to patch the bib bottom
- piece of double gauze, flannel, or cotton terry, at least 12" × 20" (30.5 × 50.8 cm) for lining

Other Supplies:

- 12" × 20" (30.5 cm × 50.8 cm) cotton batting
- water-soluble pen
- embroidery floss or pearl cotton thread
- snap fasteners, size 16— 7/16" or 1.1 cm, and pliers, or sew-on snaps (size 1 or 2) (I used a Dritz Pliers Kit.)
- basting spray, optional

CUTTING INSTRUCTIONS

- Refer to the bib pattern on page 128 and make a template. Mark "Front" and "Back" on each side of the template to know which side is the reverse. Trace the dotted lines, opening, and snap button positions from the pattern.
- Cut one 10" × 12" (25.4 × 30.5 cm) rectangle from the cotton print, for the bib top.
- Cut one 10" × 2½" (25.4 × 6.4 cm) rectangle from the linen, for the bib center.
- Cut three 3¾" x 3¾" (9.5 × 9.5 cm) squares from assorted cotton scraps, to patch the bib bottom.
- Cut one 10" × 17" (25.4 × 43.2 cm) rectangle from double gauze, for the reverse side.
- Cut one 10" × 17" (25.4 × 43.2 cm) rectangle from cotton batting.

INSTRUCTIONS

Seam allowances are ¼" (6 mm) unless otherwise noted. I recommend prewashing all fabrics to avoid shrinking. Bibs will be washed frequently!

Make the Front Bib

1. Sew together three assorted cotton scraps to create a pieced rectangle for the bib bottom. Open seams and press. Trim the pieced rectangle into a 10" × 3¾" (25.4 × 9.5 cm) rectangle.

2. Aligning raw edges, sew the pieced rectangle and linen panel together with right sides facing. Press the seam allowances to the pieced rectangle side. Repeat to add large rectangle piece to the opposite edge of the linen panel. Press the seam allowances away from the center linen panel. As shown in the diagram, both the top and bottom seams of the center linen panel are pressed away to the opposite directions.

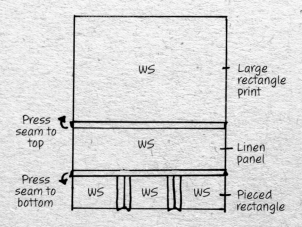

3. Using a water-soluble pen, write the baby's name or initial directly onto the center of the linen panel of the bib front.

Tip

For the pieced patch used on the front bib bottom, use up your smaller scraps for a scrappy look, or simply cut out one 10" × 3¾" (25.4 cm × 9.5 cm) rectangle from cotton print.

4. Stitch embroidery on the linen panel using backstitches. See step 2 of Embroider the Falling Rain of Raindrops Tote for backstitching instructions (page 47).

5. Spray-baste or pin the cotton batting onto the wrong side of the assembled front bib.

6. Face the assembled front bib right side up. Referring to the diagram, topstitch along the bottom edge of the top print and top edge of the pieced bottom, avoiding stitching on the linen panel.

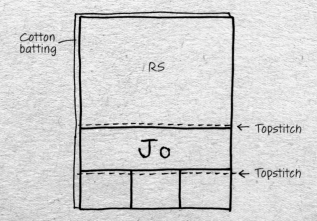

Topstitch

1. As shown in the diagram, place the *front* side of the bib template on top of the *right* side of the front bib. Align the template's dotted lines with the edges of the linen panel. Pin the template and cut out the bib.

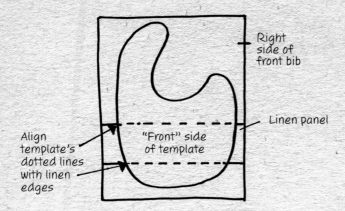

Right side of front bib

Linen panel

Align template's dotted lines with linen edges

"Front" side of template

2. Place the *back* side of the bib template on top of the *right* side of the lining. Pin the template and cut out the lining.

Assemble the Bib

1. With right sides facing, pin the front and back sides of the bib together. Sew together along the edge, leaving an opening at one side.

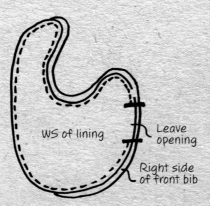

WS of lining

Leave opening

Right side of front bib

2. Press to open the seams. Using a pair of scissors, cut notches around the curves, taking care not to cut the seam.

3. Turn the bib right side out through the opening. Use a chopstick to push out the corners. Press again.

4. Pin the opening closed. Stitch closely around the entire edge of the bib, carefully catching the opening.

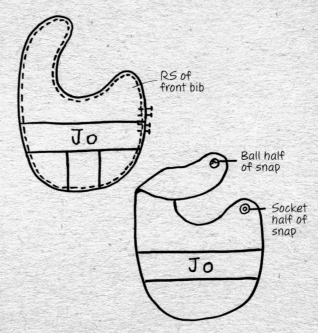

RS of front bib

Jo

Ball half of snap

Socket half of snap

Jo

Add Snap Fasteners

1. Apply snaps using the snap setter. Referring to the diagram, attach the *ball* half of the snap on the top *lining* side of the bib, and attach the *socket* half of the snap on the top *front* side of the bib. If you are sewing snaps by hand, be careful not to show the stitches on the reverse side of the bib.

BUNNY OR PANDA SOFT RING TOY

Finished size from the tip of ears to ring bottom:

3½" × 6" (8.9 × 15.2 cm) for the bunny and 3½" × 5" (8.9 × 12.7 cm) for the panda

Easily customize this soft toy to make it into a bunny or a panda by shortening or lengthening the ears and changing the eye shapes. Make it as a soft ring toy, or add several bells inside to make it a baby's rattle. The face of this toy is carefully hand-embroidered and no buttons or small parts are used for safety reasons. Use durable sewing thread, to securely stitch the opening and prevent the inside stuffing and the bells (optional) from coming out.

MATERIALS

Fabric:

To Make Bunny

- five 5" (12.7 cm) squares of different assorted prints, for ring front, ring back, head back, ears, and fringe hands
- 5" (12.7 cm) square unbleached muslin, for the front head

To Make Panda

- three 5" (12.7 cm) squares of different assorted prints, for ring front, ring back, and head back
- black-based cotton print, at least 5" × 10" (12.7 × 25.4 cm), for panda ears and fringe hands
- 5" (12.7 cm) square un-bleached muslin, for the front head

Other Supplies:

- black embroidery floss, to embroider the face
- water-soluble pen
- polyester fiberfill
- strong thread
- six jingle bells, 0.375" or 9.5 mm in diameter, to make one rattle toy, optional
- pattern transfer paper, optional
- masking tape, optional
- black permanent marker, optional

Tip

You can use colorful grosgrain ribbons to make hands instead of stitching your own hands from cotton prints.

The head and the ring body are carefully stitched together.

CUTTING INSTRUCTIONS

- Trace and cut out the pattern on page 124 to make templates for the head, ear, and ring. Trace the ear lines onto the templates.

For Bunny

- Using the bunny ear template, cut out four ears from one 5" (12.7 cm) print square.
- Cut two 2" × 4" (5.1 × 10.2 cm) rectangles from one 5" (12.7 cm) print square, for the fringe hands.
- Using the head template, cut out one oval from one 5" (12.7 cm) print square, for the head back.
- Using the head template, cut out one oval from the 5" (12.7 cm) unbleached muslin square, for the head front.
- Using the ring template, cut out two rings from two different 5" (12.7 cm) print squares, for the body.

For Panda

- Using the panda ear template, cut out four ears from the 5" × 10" (12.7 cm × 25.4 cm) black-based cotton print. From the same fabric, cut two 2" × 4" (5.1 × 10 cm) rectangles for the fringe hands.
- Using the head template, cut one oval from one 5" (12.7 cm) print square, for the head back.
- Using the head template, cut one oval from the 5" (12.7 cm) unbleached muslin square, for the head front.
- Using the ring template, cut two rings from two 5" different (12.7 cm) print squares, for the body.

INSTRUCTIONS

Seam allowances are ¼" (6 mm) unless otherwise noted. I recommend prewashing all fabrics to avoid shrinking and to make a clean toy for the baby.

Embroider the Face

1. Using the pattern transfer paper, trace the bunny or panda face onto the unbleached muslin oval following manufacturer's instructions. Or refer to step 1 of Transfer and Embroider Sashiko Design on Sashiko Style Coasters (page 104) and follow the Sunny Window method. With this method, the design is transferred using a black permanent marker, masking tape, and water-soluble pen with the sunlight from the window.

2. Embroider the face using three strands of black embroidery floss. Use satin stitches for the eyes and the nose, and use backstitches for the mouth. See the diagram for stitching the satin stitches. See step 2 of Embroider the Falling Rain of Raindrops Tote (page 47) for making backstitches.

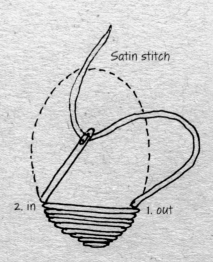

Satin stitch

2. in   1. out

Assemble the Ears and Head

1. Place one set of ears right sides together. Use a set of longer ears for the bunny and a set of shorter ears for the panda. Sew around the ear, leaving the raw edge open at the ear bottom. Carefully clip small notches along the curves, taking care not to cut the seam. Use a chopstick to turn right side out and press. Repeat to make another ear.

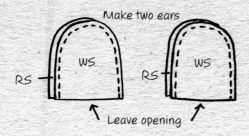

Make two ears

Leave opening

2. Fill both ears with a small amount of polyfill. Close the opening by machine-stitching ⅛" (3 mm) from the raw edges.

3. Lay the ears on the right side of the embroidered face.

For Bunny: As shown in the diagram, pin the raw edge of the ears to the right side of the head top, with the round edge of the ears placed toward the head bottom. Both ears should be placed next to each other without a space in between. Sew the ears to the head top with straight stitches across, without making curves, close to the edge. Repeat a few times to reinforce the stitches.

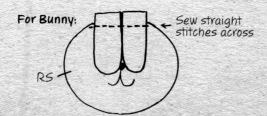

For Bunny:

Sew straight stitches across

For Panda: As shown in the diagram, pin the raw edge of the ears to both sides of the right side of the head top, following the ear lines on the template. The round edge of the ears should be placed toward the inside of the head. Sew the ears close to the edge. Repeat a few times to reinforce the stitches.

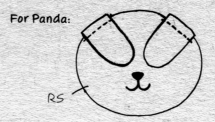

For Panda:

4. Place the heads together, right sides facing. Pin and sew around the head, leaving an opening of at least 1½" (3.8 cm) at the bottom. Carefully clip small notches along the curves. Turn the head right side out through the opening. Press the opening.

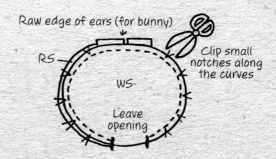

Raw edge of ears (for bunny)

Clip small notches along the curves

Leave opening

5. Stuff the head with polyfill and six jingle bells (optional). If you place bells inside, try to cover the bells with polyfill by adjusting the stuffing.

6. Using strong thread, securely hand-stitch the opening of the bunny head with tight and close stitches, making sure that the inside stuffing and the bells (optional) will not escape from the opening.

Assemble the Ring

1. Fold the 2" × 4" (5.1 × 10.2 cm) rectangle in half lengthwise, wrong sides together. Press, then unfold. Fold the long edges to meet in the center; press again. Refold in half lengthwise and match the folded edges. Topstitch along both long edges. Repeat to make the remaining fringe hand. You now have two fringe hands.

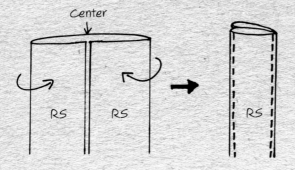

2. Fold the fringes in half, aligning the raw edges. Sew the raw edges together ⅛" (3 mm) from the edge, making a loop. Repeat for the remaining fringe.

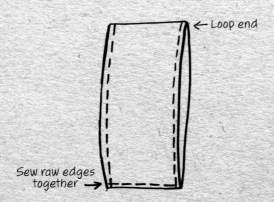

3. Position the ring front right side up, with the open ends placed at the top. Using the ring template as a guide, place the fringes onto the ring front at the marked lines. Align the raw edges of the fringes to the outer ring edge, with the fringe's loop ends facing the center of the ring. Sew the fringes in place ⅛" (3 mm) from the edge. Repeat several times to reinforce the stitches.

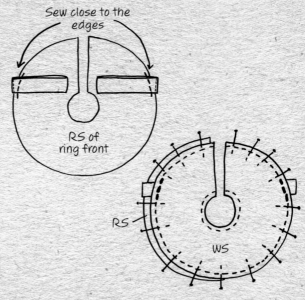

4. With right sides facing, pin the rings together. Sew around the *outer* edge, backstitching over the fringe hands for reinforcement. Leave both ends open. Repeat for the *inner* edge of the ring. When sewing the ring's *inner* edge, push away the fringe's loop ends, being careful not to catch them while machine stitching. Cut notches around the outer and inner ring, taking care not to cut the seam. Now you have sewn a curved tube with both ends open. Using a chopstick, carefully turn the tube right side out. Press.

5. Bring the two open ends together to create a loop. Using a chopstick, carefully fill the tube with polyfill from both ends. Make sure that the stuffing is packed firmly and evenly.

6. Fold under one end of the tube about ¼" (6 mm), and overlap on the remaining raw end. Pin both ends together. With strong thread, hand-stitch both ends together, covering the raw end.

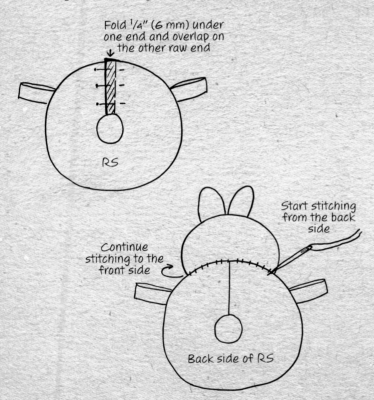

Fold ¼" (6 mm) under one end and overlap on the other raw end

RS

Start stitching from the back side

Continue stitching to the front side

Back side of RS

Assemble the Head and Ring

1. Pin the head to the ring, with about one third of the head overlapping the top part of the ring. With durable sewing thread, sew the head onto the ring body starting from the back side. Continue stitching to the front side to securely sew the head and body together.

Tip

When stitching two layers of fabrics in a circle, go slowly and stop often, rotating the fabric around the pivot point as you go. It may be helpful to mark stitching lines with a water-soluble pen, ¼" (6 mm) from the outer and inner edge, and follow those marked lines when you sew.

Panda Gift Set

The panda soft ring toy and the personalized panda bib make an adorable panda gift set for a baby.

REVERSIBLE BABY SHOES

Finished Size: *4" (10.2 cm) long and 2½" (6.4 cm) wide at the widest point*

Gentle on babies' feet and convenient for their caregivers, these fully reversible soft-sole baby shoes are made of 100 percent cotton prints and cotton batting. The shoes are made without any snaps, buttons, or exposed seams. The sole is 4" (10.2 cm) long to fit babies up to six or nine months old. Sewing small fabric pieces in curves requires some practice and patience, but it pays off when a tiny pair of shoes is finished for that precious little person! If you have difficulty sewing small parts together with a sewing machine, sew by hand instead. These shoes are not suitable for walking.

Under traditional Japanese custom, parents bring their newborn baby to a local shrine for a ceremonial blessing after the baby is one month old. The baby is usually dressed up in a baby kimono or pretty dress for the first trip to the shrine.

MATERIALS

Fabric:

- one fat quarter or 22" × 18" (55.9 × 45.7 cm) cotton print, for the exterior
- one fat quarter or 22" × 18" (55.9 × 45.7 cm) gingham check print, for lining
- one cotton print, at least 15" × 4" (38.1 × 10.2 cm) pin-dot print, for ties

Other Supplies:

- ¼ yd (0.23 m) of 45" (114.3 cm) width cotton batting
- ruler
- basting spray, optional
- water-soluble pen, optional

CUTTING INSTRUCTIONS

- Trace the patterns on page 127 to make templates for the shoes side and sole. Be sure to trace the connecting points A and B from both patterns.
- Cut two soles from cotton print (exterior).
- Cut two shoe sides from cotton print (exterior).
- Cut two soles from gingham check print (lining).
- Cut two shoe sides from gingham check print (lining).
- Cut two 14" × 1" (35.6 × 2.5 cm) strips from pin-dots prints (ties).
- Cut two soles from cotton batting.
- Cut two shoe sides from cotton batting.

INSTRUCTIONS

Seam allowances are ¼" (6 mm) unless otherwise noted.

Assemble Ties

1. Referring to the diagram, fold down ¼" (6 mm) inward on each short edge of the 14" × 1" (35.6 × 2.5 cm) strip and press both ends. Then fold the strip in half lengthwise, wrong sides together. Press and unfold. Fold the long edges to meet in the center, and press again. Topstitch along the three open edges. Repeat to make the remaining tie. Now you have two long ties.

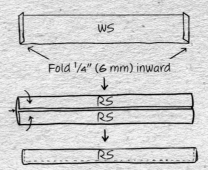

2. Cut two long ties in half at the center to create four ties measuring approximately 6¾" × ¼" (17.2 × 6 mm).

Assemble the Exterior Shoe

1. Spray-baste or pin the cotton batting to the wrong sides of the exterior shoe's side and sole. With right sides together, connect both ends of the exterior side shoe to make a loop. Pin and sew the heel ends together. Repeat for the remaining exterior piece. Open the seams and press.

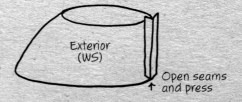

Assemble the Exterior Shoe (cont.)

2. Place the exterior sole right side up with the front sole on top and the heel at the bottom. With right sides together, connect and pin point A of the sole (tip of sole) with point A of the side shoe (tip of shoe). Then connect and pin point B of the sole (heel) with point B of the side shoe (heel). Pin and carefully sew around the entire outer edge of the sole. Cut small notches around the curves, taking care not to cut the seam. Trim the seam allowance to ⅛" (3 mm) around the sole for a smooth finish. Repeat for the remaining exterior shoe.

the ties securely to each side of the shoe opening ⅛" (3 mm) from the edges. Repeat for the remaining exterior shoe.

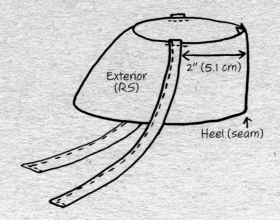

Exterior (RS)

2" (5.1 cm)

Heel (seam)

Assemble the Lining

1. Just as you did with the exterior shoes, sew the lining of the shoes. With right sides together, connect both ends of the lining's side shoe to make a loop. Pin and sew the heel ends together. Repeat for the remaining lining piece. Open the seams and press.

2. Just as you did with the exterior shoes, match point A (tip of shoe) together and point B (heel) together for both lining pieces. Using a *slightly* wider seam than the ordinary ¼" (6 mm) seam, sew around the outer edge of the sole, leaving at least 1½" (3.8 cm) opening on one side of the sole. Cut small notches around the curves, taking care not to cut the seam. Trim the excess seam allowance to ⅛" (3 mm) around the sole for a smooth finish. Repeat for the remaining shoe lining.

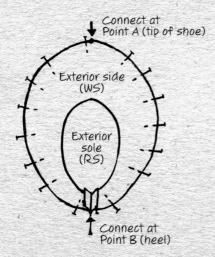

Connect at Point A (tip of shoe)

Exterior side (WS)

Exterior sole (RS)

Connect at Point B (heel)

3. Turn the exterior shoe right side out. Referring to the diagram, use a water-soluble pen (optional) to make two small marks at each side of the shoe opening, 2" (5.1 cm) from the heel seam. Align and pin the raw edges of the ties to the right side of the exterior side. Sew

Finish the Shoes

1. With right sides together, insert the shoe lining inside the exterior shoe. The ties should be tucked inside the exterior shoe, sandwiched between the lining and the exterior. Match the heel seam together for both pieces. Align the raw edges at the opening and pin. Sew carefully around the shoe opening, backstitching over ties for reinforcement. Be careful not to catch the tie ends while you go. Cut small notches around the curves of the entire shoe opening. Trim the seam allowance to ⅛" (3 mm) around the top edge for a smooth finish. Repeat for the remaining shoe.

Lining (RS)

Exterior (WS)

Tip

Using slightly wider seam allowances than the ordinary ¼" (6 mm) seam to sew the lining pieces together will make the lining just a little smaller than the exterior shoe. This will prevent the lining from becoming bulky and will help create a smooth finish for the baby's tender feet.

2. Turn the exterior shoe right side out through the opening in the lining. Push out all corners using a chopstick. Hand-stitch the opening closed.

3. Press to finish both shoes. Make a tie at front.

Here is another look of the same baby shoes. Enjoy two styles in one pair of shoes!

PUFFY PONYTAIL BOW

Finished Size: *4¼" × 3" (10.8 × 7.6 cm)*

A bow on a girl's hair is always flattering. And I mean a big puffy one! When I make these puffy bows for our girls, I let them select their own fabrics to make their favorite hair accessories. Here, I used different fabrics for the bow and the knot, but you can make one by using the same fabric, or for the knot, try using lace, velvet ribbon, or woven ribbon that is 3½" (8.9 cm) long.

MATERIALS

Fabric:

- scrap of large-scale floral fabric, at least 6" × 8" (15.2 × 20.3 cm), for bow
- scrap of small-scale floral fabric, at least 3" × 4" (7.6 × 10.2 cm), for knot

Other Supplies:

- one thick elastic hair band with no metal
- polyester fiberfill
- ½ yd (0.46 m) or 18" (45.7 cm) of ½" (1.3 cm) diameter of pompom trims, for embellishment, optional
- zipper foot for your sewing machine, optional
- fabric tube turner or loop turner, optional

CUTTING INSTRUCTIONS

- Cut one 5½" × 7" (14 × 17.8 cm) rectangle from large-scale floral fabric.
- Cut one 2" × 3½" (5.1 × 8.9 cm) rectangle from small-scale floral scrap.
- Cut pompom trims into two 8" (20.3 cm) long trims, optional.

INSTRUCTIONS

Seam allowances are ¼" (6 mm) unless otherwise noted.

Make the Bow

1. Optional embellishment: Place the large-scale fabric rectangle right side up. Pin the "ribbon" portion of the pompom trims to both sides of the longer edges, with pompoms placed toward the *inside* of the fabric. Stitch carefully along the trims close to the edges. Depending on the width of your sewing machine foot, using a zipper foot may be helpful. Cut off the pompom excess near all corners.

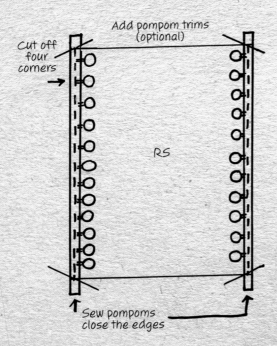

2. Fold the large-scale fabric in half widthwise, right sides together, aligning the shorter edges.

3. Sew along the edge, leaving at least 1½" (3.8 cm) opening in the center.

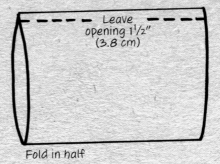

4. Open the seam and press. Roll the seam to the center of the bow, and sew both sides of the open edges together.

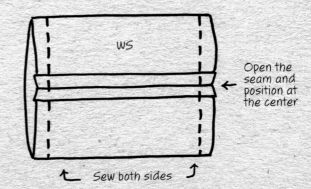

5. Trim off the four corners. Turn the bow right side out through the opening and use a chopstick to push out the corners. Stuff the bow evenly with polyester fiberfill. Do not overstuff. The bow should look soft and fluffy. Hand-stitch or machine-stitch the opening closed.

Make the Knot

1. Fold a piece of small-scale floral fabric in half lengthwise, right sides together, aligning the longer edges. Sew along the edge.

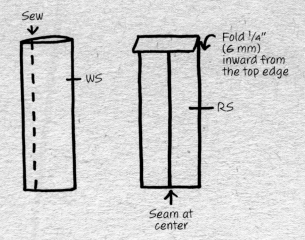

2. Turn the knot right side out. Using a fabric tube turner or loop turner may be helpful if you have one, but a chopstick will do the job. Roll the seam to the center of the knot and press. Fold the top ¼" (6 mm) inward from the top edge toward the seam line and press.

Assemble the Puffy Bow Ponytail

1. Place the bow right side up, with the seam facing the back side. Pass the elastic through the knot and wrap the knot around the bow.

2. Connect the knot ends on the back side of the bow. Using double thread, hand-stitch the knot ends together by hiding the raw edge.

Back side of the bow: Raw edges of the knots are hidden by carefully hand-stitching the knot ends together.

CHILDREN'S PENCIL BAG

Finished Size: *9½" × 5" × 1" (24.1 × 12.7 × 2.5 cm), not including the straps*

This Children's Pencil Bag is one of my favorite zakka items that I create for young children. Over the years, I've made many of these pouches for our girls and their friends, and it's been my pleasure to watch them carry my handmade pencil bags. The pouch is generously sized to hold more than a handful of pens, pencils, erasers, or even small gadgets and toys. I added a 12 mm wood bead with cotton wax cord to the zipper pull tab as an optional embellishment, but skip the wood bead if the pouch is used by children under three years of age.

MATERIALS

Fabric:

- one fat eighth or 22" × 9" (55.9 × 22.9 cm) children's themed print, for top panels

- one fat eighth or 22" × 9" (55.9 × 22.9 cm) gingham check print, for bottom panels
- one fat quarter or 22" × 18" (55.9 × 45.7 cm) pin-dot print, for straps and lining

Other Supplies:

- batting, 12" (30.5 cm) square
- 15" × 3" (38.1 × 7.6 cm) strip of fusible interfacing, to reinforce straps
- 9" (22.9 cm) zipper, color of choice
- zipper foot for your sewing machine
- basting spray, optional
- water-soluble pen
- ruler
- pins or sewing clips (I used Clover Wonder clips)
- one round wood bead, 12 mm in diameter, for zipper pull embellishment, optional
- 6" (15.2 cm) length of 1 mm or 2 mm waxed cotton cords, color of choice, for zipper pull embellishment, optional

CUTTING INSTRUCTIONS

- Cut two 10" × 3½" (25.4 × 8.9 cm) rectangles from children's themed print, for the pouch top panels.
- Cut two 10" × 2¾" (25.4 × 7 cm) rectangles from gingham check print, for the pouch bottom panels.
- Cut two 10" × 5½" (25.4 × 14 cm) rectangles from pin-dot print, for the lining.
- Cut two 14" × 2" (35.6 × 5.1 cm) strips from pin-dot print, for the straps.
- Cut two 10" × 5¾" (25.4 × 14.6 cm) rectangles from batting.
- Cut two 14" × 1" (35.6 × 2.5 cm) strips from fusible interfacing.

Tip

For a snug fit, the finished lining is designed to be slightly shorter (by ¼" or 6 mm) than the finished exterior pouch.

INSTRUCTIONS

Seam allowances are ¼" (6 mm) unless otherwise noted.

Make and Attach Straps

1. Fold the 14" × 2" (35.6 × 5.1 cm) strip of the pin-dot print fabric in half lengthwise, wrong sides together. Press and unfold. Fold both long edges to meet in the center and press. Fuse a 14" × 1" (35.6 × 2.5 cm) strip of fusible interfacing to the wrong side of the strip, centered. Then refold in half lengthwise, matching the folded edges. Pin and topstitch along both long edges. Repeat to make the remaining strap. You now have two straps that are 14" × ½" (35.6 × 1.3 cm) each. For a diagram of how to make the straps, see step 1 of Make and Add Straps of the Raindrops Tote (page 48).

2. Position the top panel right side up. Place the strap on the top panel and align both raw ends to the bottom edge. As illustrated in the diagram, position the strap's outer edges 3" (7.6 cm) away from both sides of the panel, being careful not to twist the strap. Pin the strap in place. Repeat for the remaining top panel and strap.

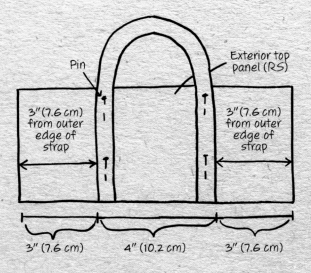

Make and Attach Straps (cont.)

3. Using a water-soluble pen and a ruler, mark two vertical lines across both strap ends, 1¼" (3.2 cm) from the bottom edge. Repeat for the remaining strap. These lines indicate where the topstitch lines of straps will stop in the next step.

4. Sew the strap to the top panel. As illustrated in the diagram, topstitch both ends of the strap in place. Starting from the bottom edge, stitch upward and across the marked line; then return back to the bottom edge, sewing in a reverse U-shape. After stitching both ends of the strap to the top panel, repeat to attach the other strap to the remaining top panel.

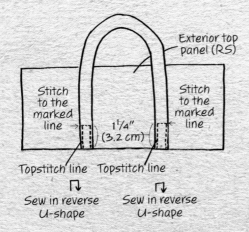

5. With right sides together, align the bottom edge of the top panel and the top edge of the bottom panel. The strap ends should be caught under the seam of the joined pieces. Pin and sew both pieces together, backstitching over the straps for reinforcement. Press the seams *down* toward the bottom panel. Repeat for the remaining panels.

6. Spray-baste or pin the batting to the wrong side of the pieced panel. Topstitch along the top edge of the bottom panel, as illustrated. Repeat for the remaining pieced panel.

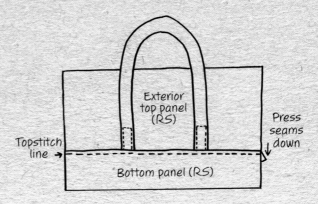

Sew the Zipper

1. Change the sewing machine foot to zipper foot. Attach the 9" (22.9 cm) zipper to the top edge of the exterior and the lining pieces. Refer to steps 1-4 of Sew the Zipper of Kotori Zipper Pouch (page 42) for directions on attaching a zipper.

Tip

When sewing the zipper, bring both straps down to the bottom edge of the exterior panels, away from the zipper. Using pins or sewing clips to hold both straps to the bottom edge of the panels will be helpful.

Finish the Pouch

1. Change the sewing machine foot back to the regular sewing foot. Bring both pieces of the exterior to one side and both pieces of the lining to the other side. Unzip the zipper all the way open and place the straps inside the lining to keep them out of the way. With right sides together, pin around the entire pieces, leaving a 4" (10.2 cm) opening at the bottom of the lining. Ensure that the teeth of both zipper ends are facing toward the *exterior* fabrics. Sew around all sides, starting from the bot-tom of the lining.

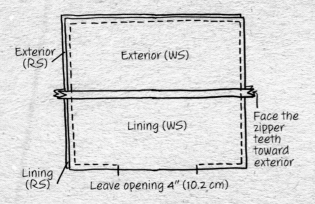

Exterior (RS)

Exterior (WS)

Lining (WS)

Face the zipper teeth toward exterior

Lining (RS)

Leave opening 4" (10.2 cm)

2. Form bottom corners of the exterior and the lining. Match the bottom seam line of the exterior to the side seam line and make a flattened triangle. Using a ruler and pencil, draw a line 1" (2.5 cm) across the triangle. Sew along the marked line and trim the excess, leaving a ¼" (6 mm) seam allowances. Repeat for the remaining exterior and the lining. Refer to the diagram in step 4 of Assemble the Exterior Bag for the Bento Lunch Bag (page 108) on forming bottom corners.

3. Turn the pouch right side out from the opening of the lining. Hand-stitch or machine-stitch to close the opening. Press the entire pouch for a neat finish.

Optional: Zipper Embellishment

1. Pass the 6" (15.2 cm) cotton wax cord through the hole of the zipper pull tab. Fold the cord in half to make a loop and match both raw ends together. Thread through the 12 mm wood bead. Tie the cord ends together tightly to secure the knot. Cut off the excess cords.

For Variation

For a boy's version of the carrying pouch, I used fabrics with bold prints of automobiles.

HANDMADE KITCHEN ZAKKA

Every day, I enjoy spending time in our kitchen. I prepare tea, cook, and eat meals with my family, help with our kids' homework, chat with my friends and family, listen to the radio, read newspapers, and enjoy a glass of wine. It is the heart of our house and that's why I like to create handmade zakka items for the kitchen that are both charming and practical. I hope these kitchen zakka items make your time spent in the kitchen more enjoyable, too.

AIRMAIL MUG RUG

Finished Size: *10" × 8" (25.4 × 20.3 cm)*

We live in the Internet age, yet I still enjoy exchanging airmail with my family and friends living in Japan. For this zakka project, I created an airmail envelope-style mug rug by cutting up small fabric motifs into postage stamp shapes and stitching them onto a linen panel with machine appliqué. Hand-embroider or use alphabet stamps to add a name, street address, or a short message to the mailing label located at the bottom right corner. If you choose, stamp travel and postage-themed rubber stamps using fabric ink to the front of the airmail that crossed the ocean to be delivered!

- scrap of ivory linen, at least 5" (12.7 cm) square, for mailing label
- scraps of assorted fabric with small motifs, to create postage stamps
- scrap of unbleached muslin, at least 9" (22.9 cm) square, to create white postage stamp frames

Other Supplies:

- 11" × 9" (27.9 cm × 22.9 cm) insulated batting (I used Insul-Bright)
- ¼" yd (0.23 m) lightweight paper-backed fusible web, to fuse postage stamps and mailing label (I used HeatnBond Lite)
- pinking shears
- water-soluble pen
- ruler

MATERIALS

Fabric:

- one fat eighth or 22" × 9" (55.9 × 22.9 cm) medium-weight linen, for front panel
- one fat eighth or 22" × 9" (55.9 × 22.9 cm) fabric, for backing
- one fat quarter or 22" × 18" (55.9 × 45.7 cm) print fabric for binding. Select a print fabric with red, white, and blue colors, to create the air-mail envelope borders. Otherwise use red or blue fabrics with white dots, borders, or plaids to frame the envelope.

- one business card or cardboard paper cut into 3½" × 2" (8.9 × 5.1 cm) rectangle, for mailing label ironing template
- embroidery floss or pearl cotton thread, optional
- alphabet stamps, optional
- travel and airmail themed stamps, optional (I used Par Avion Rubber Stamps from Cavallini & Co.)
- fabric ink, black and red, optional
- basting spray, optional
- walking foot of sewing machine, optional

CUTTING INSTRUCTIONS

- Cut one 10½" × 8½" (26.9 × 21.6 cm) linen panel from medium-weight linen.
- Cut one 11" × 9" (27.9 × 22.9 cm) rectangle from backing fabric.
- Cut two 22" × 2½" (55.9 × 6.4 cm) strips from red, white, and blue binding fabric. (I cut mine on bias to create a lattice pattern of the checkered fabric, but cutting on bias is not necessary.)
- Cut one 4¼" × 2¾" (10.8 × 7 cm) rectangle from red, white, and blue binding fabric for mailing label frame.
- Cut one 4½" × 3" (11.4 × 7.6 cm) rectangle from ivory linen scrap.

INSTRUCTIONS

Seam allowances are ¼" (6 mm) unless otherwise noted.

Embellish the Front Panel

1. Create postage stamps. Cut out the selected small motifs from your stash by adding at least ¾" (1.9 cm) seam around the motif design. Following the manufacturer's instructions, iron the paper-backed fusible web onto the wrong side of the selected motifs. For motifs with white background, cut out the motif into postage stamp shapes using pinking shears. Stamps can be in rectangle, square, round, oval, or any shape of your choice, based on the design of the selected motif.

Motif with white background backed with fusible web

Cut out motif

Unbleached muslin

2. For motifs with non-white background, create a postage-stamp look by framing with unbleached muslin frame. Apply paper-backed fusible web to the wrong side of the selected motifs, as described in step 1. Cut out these motifs into shapes of your choice using *regular* scissors. Cut unbleached muslin at least ½" (1.3 cm) larger than the motif. Peel off the paper backing of the motif and fuse to the center of the muslin. Then iron paper-backed fusible web onto the wrong side of the muslin. Using pinking shears, cut around the muslin edge to create postage-stamp shape.

Embellish the Front Panel (cont.)

3. Repeat steps 1 and 2 until you have enough postage stamps to embellish the front linen panel.

4. Create a frame for the mailing label. Iron the paper-backed fusible web onto the wrong side of the 4¼" × 2¾" (10.8 × 7 cm) red, white, and blue print rectangle. Using pinking shears, cut the frame to 4" × 2½" (10.2 × 6.4 cm).

5. Fuse the mailing label frame to the bottom right corner of the linen panel, approximately 1" (2.5 cm) from the corner.

6. Arrange the cutout postage stamps on the front linen panel as desired, leaving at least 1" (2.5 cm) around the panel. Slightly overlap the corners of several postage stamps, as I did with my mug rug. If you plan to stamp Airmail or other travel-related rubber stamps to the panel, leave space for the stamps. After arranging the postage stamps as desired, peel off the paper backing of the stamps and press in place with an iron.

7. If desired, ink the travel themed stamps with fabric ink, and stamp them onto the panel. Allow the ink to dry and heat set with a hot iron.

8. Layer the embellished linen panel right side up over the insulated batting. If desired, pin or spray-baste the fabrics together. Using white or matching colored thread, topstitch around the stamps and mailing label frame just inside the pinked edges. For layered stamps, also topstitch close to the edges of the center motif.

Tip

Quilting with a walking foot really makes a difference! It prevents the fabrics from shifting and helps you sew through layers of fabrics with ease.

Machine-Quilt the Mug Rug

1. Make a quilt sandwich of the backing, insulated batting, and embellished linen panel. Use basting spray or pins to attach the backing fabric. Using a water-soluble pen and a ruler, draw a straight line from the top to the bottom in the center of the linen panel. Continue to draw parallel lines side to side of the linen panel, with the lines ½" (1.3 cm) apart from each other.

2. If desired, change the sewing machine foot to walking foot. Sew through three layers of fabrics based on the drawn lines, beginning from the center line and working your way out.

3. Trim the edges to a 10" × 8" (25.4 × 20.3 cm) rectangle. Change the sewing machine foot back to the regular foot.

Embellish the Mailing Label

1. Using a business card as an ironing template, fold and press four edges of the 4½" × 3" (11.4 × 7.6 cm) ivory linen rectangle inward, to create a label. The pressed label should measure 3½" × 2" (8.9 × 5.1 cm).

2. Hand-stitch or use alphabet stamps to embellish the mailing label with a short message, name, or address. I hand-embroidered three ruled lines using running stitches and stitched the gift recipient's name using backstitches.

3. Pin the embellished mailing label to the center of the mailing label frame. Top-stitch the label in place close to the edges.

Finish the Mug Rug

1. Create a double-fold binding strip, following diagram (1). With right sides together, join two 22" × 2½" (55.9 × 6.4 cm) strips perpendicular to each other. Draw a diagonal line using a ruler and a pencil. Pin and stitch along the marked line at a 90 degree angle to join the strips together (A). Trim and press the seam open (B). With wrong sides together, fold one short end of the strip in a right angle and trim the excess, leaving ¼" (6 mm) seam allowances (C). Then fold the strip in half lengthwise, wrong sides together and press (D). Now you have a double binding strip that is approximately 42" long (106.7 cm).

2. Pin the folded edge of the binding strip to the center of one edge of the front panel, aligning the raw edges. Leave 3" (7.6 cm) of binding unsewn at the beginning and start stitching. Stop stitching when you are ¼" (6 mm) from the first corner. Backstitch to reinforce the stitches. Refer to diagram (2).

3. Miter the corners. Fold the binding strip upward at a 45 degree angle, creating a diagonal fold (A). Fold the strip back down to create a mitered corner (B). Align the raw edges and

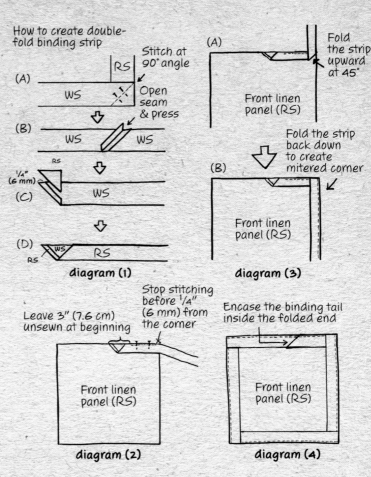

How to create double-fold binding strip

diagram (1)

diagram (2)

diagram (3)

diagram (4)

pin. Starting from the top edge, begin sewing along the binding's edge. Continue to stitch around the entire edge of the mug rug, mitering all corners. Refer to diagram (3).

4. When you return to the starting point, encase the raw end of the binding tail inside the folded end. Pin and finish stitching until you reach the starting point. Refer to diagram (4).

5. Fold the binding toward the back of the quilt. Pin to hold in place. Miter all corners. Using matching thread, hand-stitch the binding to the backing fabric.

SASHIKO STYLE COASTERS

Finished Size: *4½" (11.4 cm) square*

Sashiko is a traditional Japanese stitching technique that originated to mend and reuse textiles during a period when fabrics were very scarce and valuable. The clothes were strengthened with a series of running stitches for daily wear and tear and often layers of fabrics were patched together to add durability and warmth. For these coasters, I designed the symmetrical hearts pattern, inspired by folklore motifs, and stitched on natural linen to add the zakka taste to this Japanese classical needlework. When transferring the embroidery design to linen, you can use pattern transfer papers or simply use the sunny window method as described on page 104.

MATERIALS

Fabric:

- scrap of natural color linen, 5" (12.7 cm) square
- scrap of cotton print, 5" (12.7 cm) square, for the reverse side

Other Supplies:

- 1¾" (4.5 cm) length ½" (1.3 cm) ribbon, for the side embellishment
- scrap of batting, 5" (12.7 cm) square
- embroidery floss or pearl cotton threads in various colors (I used DMC Pearl Cotton size 5, for its volume and durability)

- pattern transfer paper, optional
- water-soluble pen, optional
- black permanent marker, optional
- masking tape, optional
- basting spray, optional

The traditional sashiko patterns are designed with geometric and repetitive patterns in shapes of diamonds, hemp leaves, persimmon flowers, ocean waves, rice fields, tortoise shells, and more.

INSTRUCTIONS

Seam allowances are ¼" (6 mm) unless otherwise noted.

Transfer and Embroider Sashiko Design

1. Using the pattern transfer paper, follow the manufacturer's instructions and trace the sashiko embroidery design to the linen square. Or, use the sunny window method as follows: Trace the sashiko embroidery pattern on page 126 onto a 5" (12.7 cm) square piece of tracing paper with a pencil, centered. Then trace the pencil lines with a black permanent marker to make the lines more noticeable. Using masking tape, securely tape the traced paper design onto the window or glass door with sunlight coming in. Then, tape the linen square on top of the traced paper and trace the design onto the fabric with a water-soluble pen.

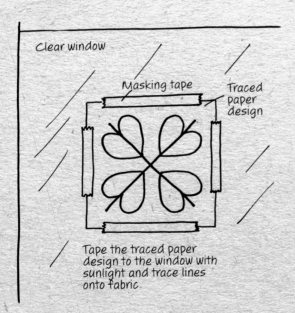

Tape the traced paper design to the window with sunlight and trace lines onto fabric.

2. Embroider the pattern onto the linen square with sashiko running stitches. In traditional sashiko running stitches, the topstitch lengths are slightly longer than the bottom stitches, with a ratio of 3:2. Refer to the diagram.

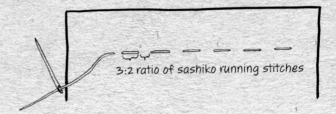

3:2 ratio of sashiko running stitches

Assemble the Coaster

1. Spray-baste or pin the batting onto the wrong side of the embroidered linen square.

2. Fold the 1¾" (4.5 cm) piece of ½" (1.3 cm) ribbon in half widthwise. Sew the ribbon ends together close to the edge to make a loop.

3. Aligning the raw edges, position the ribbon ends on top of the right side of the linen square, ¾" (1.9 cm) from the top edge, with loop ends pointing toward the inside of the square. Refer to the diagram. Pin and sew in place ⅛" (3 mm) from the edges, going back and forth to reinforce the stitches.

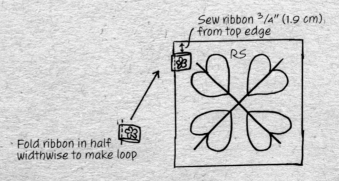

Sew ribbon ¾" (1.9 cm) from top edge

RS

Fold ribbon in half widthwise to make loop

4. With right sides facing, pin the batting, linen square, and backing fabric together. Sew around all four edges, leaving at least a 2" (5.1 cm) opening on one side. Press to open the seams. Trim the four corners.

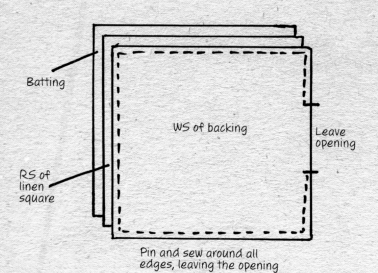

Batting

WS of backing

Leave opening

RS of linen square

Pin and sew around all edges, leaving the opening

5. Turn the coaster right side out through the opening and use a chopstick to push out the corners. Press again. Hand-stitch the opening closed.

For Variation:

Classic sashiko projects are often worked on indigo fabric using white threads. These coasters are stitched on navy linen with colorful threads as alternate fabric options to resemble the traditional look.

INSULATED BENTO LUNCH BAG

Finished Size: *13" × 7½" × 5" (33 × 19 × 12.7 cm)*

The term *bento* in Japanese refers to a home-cooked or takeout meal packed in a lunch box. Japanese-style bento is typically carried in a bento bag—a compact lunch bag that closes with a drawstring. For this Insulated Bento Lunch Bag, the layer of insulated lining is sewn between the exterior bag and lining to help keep the food hot or cold. Make a matching Wrap-Around Chopsticks Holder (page 112) to complete the lunch set. This versatile bag can be used as a small tote to carry other items, too.

MATERIALS

Fabric:

- ½ yd (0.46 m) or 44" × 18" (111.8 × 45.7 cm) of medium-weight cotton print, for exterior bag

- ½ yd (0.46 m) or 44" × 18" (111.8 × 45.7 cm) of navy and white polka dot print, for lining

- ¼ yd (0.23 m) or 44" × 9" (111.8 × 22.9 cm) of gingham check print, for top closure panels

- scrap of print fabric, to create original fabric label, optional

- ½ yd (0.46 m) or 44" × 18" (111.8 × 45.7 cm) insulated lining (I used Insul-Bright)

Other Supplies:

- 24" (61 cm) length of 1¼" (3.2 cm) width heavy cotton webbing, for straps

- 64" (162.6 cm) length of cotton or acrylic cord, for drawstring

- ruler and pencil

- pins or sewing clips, optional (I used Clover Wonder Clips)

- large safety pin or bodkin, to thread cords through the bag opening

- small amount of polyester fiberfill, to add embellished balls at cord ends, optional

From preschoolers to the elders, bringing their home-cooked meal packed in a boxy lunch box or *bento* box to school, work, and leisure is a Japanese tradition. Delicious and nutritiously balanced, *bento* carried in a *bento* bag is a healthy and money-saving way of fixing lunch in Japan.

CUTTING INSTRUCTIONS

- Cut two 14" × 11" (35.6 × 27.9 cm) rectangles from medium-weight cotton print, for exterior bag.

- Cut two 14" × 11" (35.6 × 27.9 cm) rectangles from navy and white polka-dot print, for lining.

- Cut two 14½" × 7" (36.8 × 17.8 cm) rectangles from gingham check print, for top closure panels.

- Cut two 14" × 11" (35.6 × 27.9 cm) rectangles from insulated lining.

- Cut two 12" (30.5 cm) lengths of heavy cotton webbing.

- Cut two 32" (81.3 cm) lengths of cotton or acrylic cord, for drawstrings.

Tip

Instead of using a fabric scrap, make an original linen label. Using permanent ink, stamp your favorite stamp onto a linen scrap and heat set with a hot iron. Fold and press all four edges of the linen label inward. Stitch the label onto the bag.

INSTRUCTIONS

Seam allowances are ¼" (6 mm) unless otherwise noted.

Assemble the Exterior Bag

1. Pin the insulated lining piece to the wrong side of 14" × 11" (35.6 × 27.9 cm) medium-weight cotton print rectangle. Using sewing clips is helpful when holding thick layers of fabrics together, instead of regular pins. Set your sewing machine stitch length to a long stitch. Machine-baste or sew both layers together in long stitches, using ⅛" (3 mm) seam allowances. Do not backstitch. Repeat to machine-baste the remaining insulated lining to another exterior fabric.

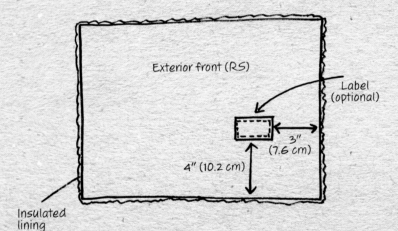

Exterior front (RS)

Label (optional)

3" (7.6 cm)

4" (10.2 cm)

Insulated lining

2. **Optional:** Add your own fabric label. Cut out any small motif of your choice from print fabric and leave at least ½" (1.3 cm) of allowance around the motif. Fold and press all four edges of the cut out motif inward to create label. Position the label at the bottom right corner of the right side of the front exterior panel. Pin the label 3" (7.6 cm) in from the side edge and 4" (10.2 cm) up from the bottom edge. Sew the label using matching colored machine thread.

Exterior (RS)

Exterior (WS)

Stitch around three edges

Insulated lining

Tip

Make your own straps from two 4" × 12" (10.2 × 30.5 cm) strips of coordinating fabric and two 2" × 12" (5.1 × 30.5 cm) strips of batting or interfacing. Refer to step 1 on page 48 for instructions for making straps.

3. With right sides facing, pin and sew both short sides and the bottom edge of the basted exterior rectangles together, leaving the top unsewn. Carefully press the seams open, using the tip of the iron.

4. Form bottom corners of the bag. Match bottom seam line to side seam line and make a flattened triangle. Using a ruler and pencil, draw a line 5"(12.7 cm) across the triangle, as shown in the diagram. Sew along the marked line and trim the excess, leaving a ¼" (6 mm) seam allowances. Repeat for the other bottom corner of the exterior bag.

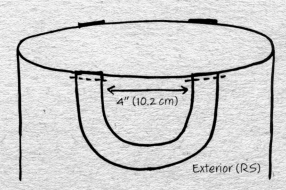

4" (10.2 cm)

Exterior (RS)

5. Pin both ends of one strap to the top edge of the right side of the exterior bag front, aligning the raw edges. Center the strap with 4" (10.2 cm) between the ends. Stitch the strap end approximately ⅛" (3 mm) from the top edge. Repeat with the other strap and bag back.

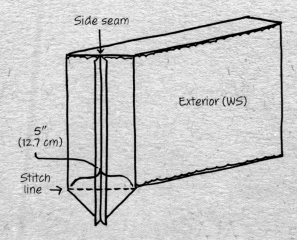

Side seam

Exterior (WS)

5"
(12.7 cm)

Stitch line →

Assemble the Bag Lining

1. Just as you assembled the exterior bag, sew the bag lining together using two panels of 14" × 11" (35.6 × 27.9 cm) navy and white polka-dot print, leaving at least a 4" (10 cm) opening on one side of the bag lining for turning. Press the seams open.

2. Form bottom corners of the bag lining as you did with the exterior bag.

Assemble the Top Closure

1. With right sides facing, pin and sew the short sides of the 14½" × 7" (36.8 × 17.6 cm) pink and white gingham check top closure panels together, using ½" (1.3 cm) seam allowances. Securely backstitch the beginning and end stitches for reinforcement. Leave 2" (5.1 cm) from the top edge unsewn for both sides.

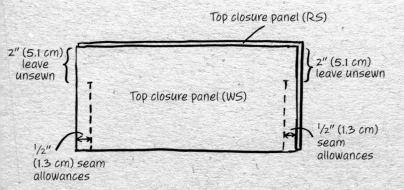

Top closure panel (RS)

2" (5.1 cm) leave unsewn

Top closure panel (WS)

2" (5.1 cm) leave unsewn

½" (1.3 cm) seam allowances

½" (1.3 cm) seam allowances

2. Create a double-folded seam for both short sides. Press and open ½" (1.3 cm) seam on both short sides of the 14½" × 7" (36.8 × 17.6 cm) top closure panels. For each seam, press under another ¼" (6 mm) inward to create

double-folded seam. Topstitch along the folded edge, from the wrong side of panel.

3. Create casings. Fold and press under the top edge by ¼" (6 mm) inward to the wrong side of the top closure panels. Then fold and press under another ¾" (1.9 cm), to make a double fold from the top edge. Pin and sew along the edge of the bottom fold. Repeat for the other side of the top closure. Now you have a casing for the drawstring cords to pass around the entire bag opening.

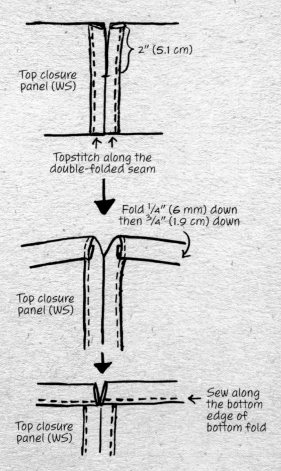

2" (5.1 cm)

Top closure panel (WS)

Topstitch along the double-folded seam

Fold ¼" (6 mm) down then ¾" (1.9 cm) down

Top closure panel (WS)

Top closure panel (WS)

Sew along the bottom edge of bottom fold

Finish the Bag

1. With right sides together, insert the top closure inside the exterior bag and match the side seams together. Align raw edges at the top. The straps should be sandwiched between the exterior bag and the top closure.

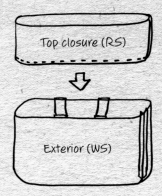

2. Insert the lining into the exterior bag, facing right sides together. Align and pin the raw edges and the seams of all three pieces together, from the exterior side: exterior bag, top closure, and bag lining. Use sewing clips or pins to hold all three pieces together at the bag opening. Sew around the upper edges of the bag, backstitching over the straps for reinforcement.

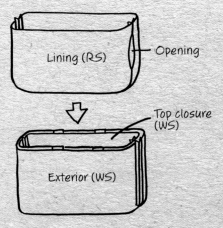

3. Turn the bag, top closure, and lining right side out through the opening in the lining. Hand-stitch or machine-stitch the opening closed.

4. Press around the top edge of the bag opening for a clean finish. Pull the top closure and the straps away from the opening. Referring to the diagram, topstitch around the upper edge of the bag with matching machine thread.

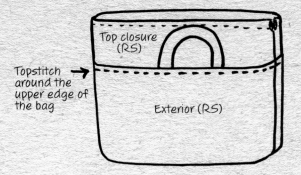

5. Using a large safety pin or bodkin, thread one cord into the casing and pass the cord all the way around and return to where you started. Tie the knot ends securely together. Thread the remaining cord through the other casing, and repeat.

   Optional: Add embellished balls at the cord ends. Refer to the Make the Embellished Ball of Wrap Around Chopsticks Holder (page 114) to create two embellished balls using fabric remnants and small amount of polyester fiber-fill. Securely stitch the balls to both cord ends.

WRAP-AROUND CHOPSTICKS HOLDER

Finished Size: *15" × 9½" (38 × 24 cm) when opened*

Say good-bye to disposable chopsticks and plastic cutlery by carrying this convenient holder in your lunch box. This is a traditional Japanese-style chopsticks holder that is eco-friendly and easy to sew. Great for chopsticks, it can also hold forks and spoons, crochet hooks, knitting needles, color pencils, or any long and narrow objects up to approximately 11" (27.9 cm) long. The holder stores the contents securely inside by wrapping around the cords tightly and tucking the cute embellished ball under the cords. Two coordinating fabrics of 15" (38.1 cm) squares will make two sets of chopsticks holders, or a single 15" (38 cm) square will make one chopsticks holder. The exterior and lining fabrics will be the same if the holder is made from one 15" (38.1 cm) square.

MATERIALS

Fabric:

- two coordinating fat quarters, or 22" × 18" (55.9 × 45.7 cm) each, for the exterior, lining, and embellished balls

Other Supplies:

- one 21" (53.3 cm) length cotton or acrylic cord
- ruler and a cutting mat
- small amount of polyester fiberfill
- strong thread, to securely sew the embellished ball (I used pearl cotton thread.)

Japanese chopsticks have pointed ends that help pick up beans, noodles, fish, rice, and vegetables. The chopsticks for men, women, and children usually come in different lengths, with men's chopsticks being the longest, measuring 9"–10" (22.9–25.4 cm) and the children's chopsticks being the shortest, measuring as short as 5½" (14 cm).

CUTTING INSTRUCTIONS

- For exterior and lining: Using a ruler and a cutting mat, cut two coordinating fabrics precisely into 15" (38.1 cm) squares. Then cut the squares diagonally in half, creating two half square triangles for each square (total of four triangles). You will use two coordinating triangles, one from each fabric, to create one chopsticks holder.

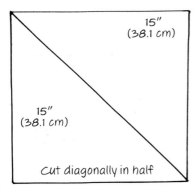

Cut diagonally in half

- For the embellished ball, cut out a 2" (5.1 cm) diameter circle from a piece of firm cardboard, such as cereal box, to make a template for the embellished ball. Tracing a small jar lid or a small container cup may be helpful. The cutting of this circle does not need to be very precise. Using the template cut out two circles from remnant fabric.

INSTRUCTIONS

Seam allowances are ¼" (6 mm) unless otherwise noted.

Make the Embellished Ball

1. Fold the 21" (53.3 cm) length of cord in half and tie both cord ends tightly together to make a knot. Cut off the excess cord ends.

2. Using craft thread, sew a running stitch all around the 2" (5.1 cm) diameter circle with ¼" (6 mm) seam allowances. Gently pull the thread ends with right side out. Hide the raw edges inside the small hole in the middle. Do not cut thread.

3. Place the knot end of the cord inside the small hole, and stuff a small amount of polyfill to add softness. Using the tip of a chopstick or any pointy object, gently push the edges inside the ball. Pull the thread tightly to form a gathered ball. Sew a couple of stitches to secure the gather; then knot and trim the thread.

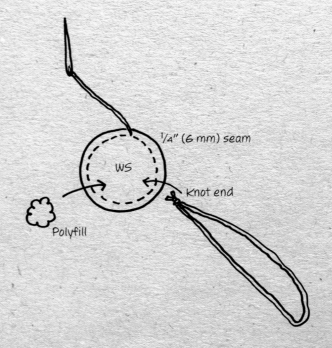

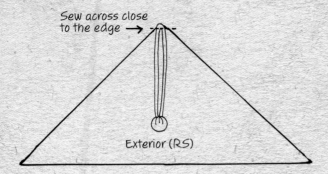

Sew across close to the edge →

Exterior (RS)

Assemble the Chopsticks Holder

1. Place the exterior triangle right side up with the longest side at bottom. Align the loop end of the cord and the top peak of the right side of the exterior triangle. Pin and sew straight stitches across close to the edge, going back and forth to reinforce the stitches.

2. With right sides facing, pin the exterior triangle and the lining triangle together. Sew around all three sides, leaving a 3" (7.6 cm) opening at the center of the longest side. When you reach the corner where the loop end is sewn in between, sew straight stitches back and forth to secure the cord ends. Press to open seams using a tip of the iron. Trim three corners.

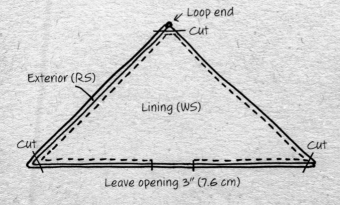

Loop end

Cut

Exterior (RS)

Lining (WS)

Cut

Cut

Leave opening 3" (7.6 cm)

3. Turn the triangles right side out through the opening. Use a chopstick to gently push out the corners, being careful not to poke through the fabric. Press all edges and corners neatly.

4. Place the *lining* side right side up. Fold over the left corner of the triangle 5" (12.7 cm) toward the inside, aligning the bottom edges.

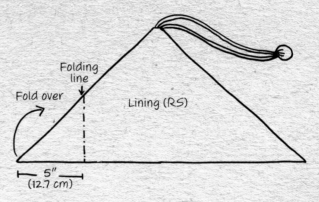

Folding line

Fold over

Lining (RS)

5"
(12.7 cm)

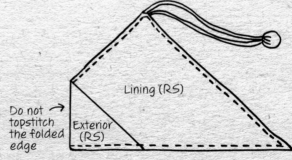

Lining (RS)

Do not → topstitch the folded edge

Exterior (RS)

5. Using matching machine thread, topstitch ⅛" (3 mm) from the edges, avoiding the folded edge. Carefully catch the opening while you sew.

6. Using the remaining half square triangles, you can make another chopsticks holder by repeating the above steps.

HOW TO USE THE CHOPSTICKS HOLDER

1. Place the pointed ends of your chopsticks inside the pocket.

2. Fold over the other end.

3. Roll the holder from bottom up.

4. Wrap around the cords and tuck the embellished ball underneath the cords.

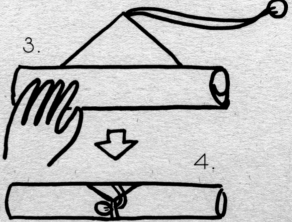

Matching Lunch Set

Create Insulated Bento Lunch Bag and the Wrap-Around Chopsticks Holder using coordinating fabrics to make a matching lunch set.

CUTLERY CARRIER

Finished Size: *9½" × 3" × 2½" (24.1 × 7.6 × 7 cm), not including the straps*

This Cutlery Carrier nicely stores cutlery and chopsticks in our kitchen. With the attached straps, it can easily travel to the dining area, living room, or to our backyard table with convenience. The container can also be used at the work desk or sewing table to sort stationery items and craft supplies neatly. Use heavy cotton or home décor–weight fabric for the exterior and use medium-weight linen for the lining. The container is fully lined with batting to add softness and support.

MATERIALS

Fabric:

- one fat eighth or 22" × 9" (55.9 × 22.9 cm) heavy cotton print or home décor–weight material, for exterior and straps
- one fat eighth or 22" × 9" (55.9 × 22.9 cm) medium-weight linen, for lining

Other Supplies:

- batting, 14" × 10" (35.6 × 25.4 cm)
- basting spray, optional
- ruler
- pencil

CUTTING INSTRUCTIONS

- Cut one 13" × 9" (33 × 22.9 cm) rectangle from heavy cotton print.
- Cut two 7¾" × 2" (19.7 × 5.1 cm) strips from heavy cotton print.
- Cut one 13" × 8¾" (33 × 22.2 cm) rectangle from medium-weight linen.
- Cut one 13" × 9" (33 × 22. cm) rectangle from batting.

Tip

The lining is intentionally shorter than the exterior by ¼" (6 mm) so the lining will fit smoothly inside the exterior container.

The container stores craft supplies neatly at your sewing area.

INSTRUCTIONS

Seam allowances are ¼" (6 mm) unless otherwise noted.

Make and Attach Straps

1. Fold the 7¾" × 2" (19.7 × 5.1 cm) strip of heavy cotton fabric in half lengthwise, wrong sides together, and press. Then fold the long edges to meet in the center and press again. Pin and topstitch ⅛" (3 mm) from both long edges. Repeat to make the remaining strap. You now have two straps that are each 7¾" × ½" (19.7 × 1.3 cm) long. For diagram on making the straps, refer to step 1 of Make and Add Straps of Simple Linen Tote (page 48), but do not fuse interfacing or batting to these straps.

2. Spray-baste or pin the batting to the wrong side of the 13" × 9" (33 × 22.9 cm) exterior rectangle. Pin the strap's raw ends to the right side of the long edge of the exterior rectangle, centered, with 3" (7.6 cm) between both ends. Machine-baste the strap ends ⅛" (3 mm) from the top edge. Repeat to attach the remaining strap to the other long edge of the rectangle.

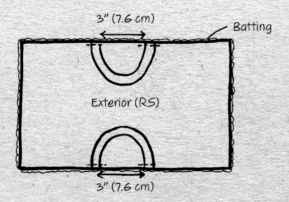

Assemble the Exterior

1. Fold the exterior panel in half lengthwise, with right sides facing. Pin and sew together both short sides of the panel, leaving the top opening unsewn. Carefully press the seams open using the tip of an iron.

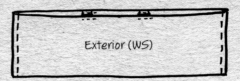

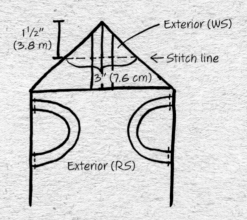

2. To form flat bottom corners, make a flattened triangle at one corner so that the bottom of the exterior is lying flat against the side, as illustrated. Measure 1½" (3.8 cm) from the peak of the corner and make a mark. Using a ruler and a pencil, draw a 3" (7.6 cm) straight line across the triangle, 1½" (3.8 cm) away from the peak of the corner. Sew along the marked line and trim the excess, leaving ¼" (6 mm) seam allowances. Repeat for the remaining bottom corner of the exterior.

Assemble the Lining

1. Just as you assembled the exterior, sew the lining using the 13" × 8¾" (33 × 22.2 cm) medium-weight linen rectangle. Form flat bottom corners of the lining, as you did with the exterior.

Finish the Container

1. With right sides together, insert the lining inside the exterior and match the side seams. Align and pin the raw edges at the top. Both straps should be sandwiched between the exterior and the lining. Sew around the upper edge, leaving at least a 2" (5.1 cm) opening for turning. Backstitch over the straps for reinforcement.

2. Turn the container right side out through the opening at the top edge. Insert the lining back into the exterior and press around the opening for a clean finish. Topstitch around the upper edge of the container with ⅛" (3 mm) from the edge, catching the opening closed.

3. Press the ends from the exterior side to form a box shape. As illustrated, topstitch top-down along two corners of the exterior to form a neat box bottom, making sure that the container's depth measures 3" (7.6 cm) across at both the top and the bottom edge, as illustrated. Repeat for the remaining two corners.

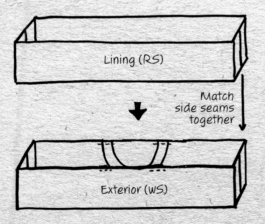

Lining (RS)

Match side seams together

Exterior (WS)

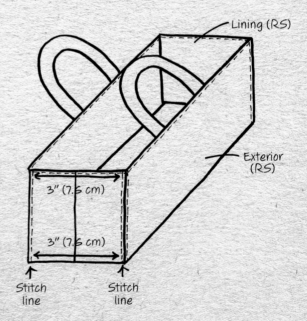

Lining (RS)

Exterior (RS)

3" (7.6 cm)

3" (7.6 cm)

Stitch line

Stitch line

PATTERNS

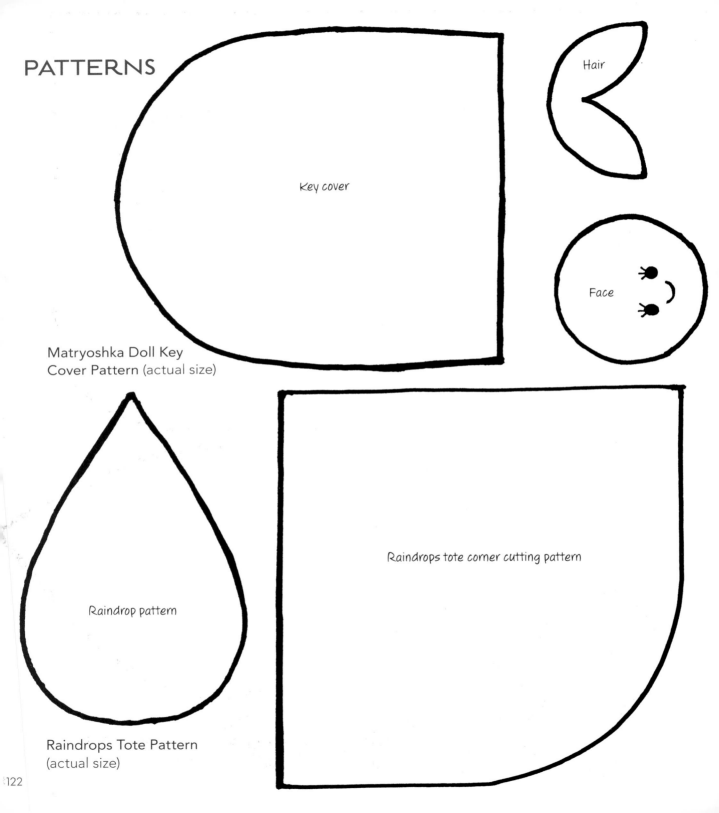

Hair

Key cover

Face

Matryoshka Doll Key
Cover Pattern (actual size)

Raindrop pattern

Raindrops tote corner cutting pattern

Raindrops Tote Pattern
(actual size)

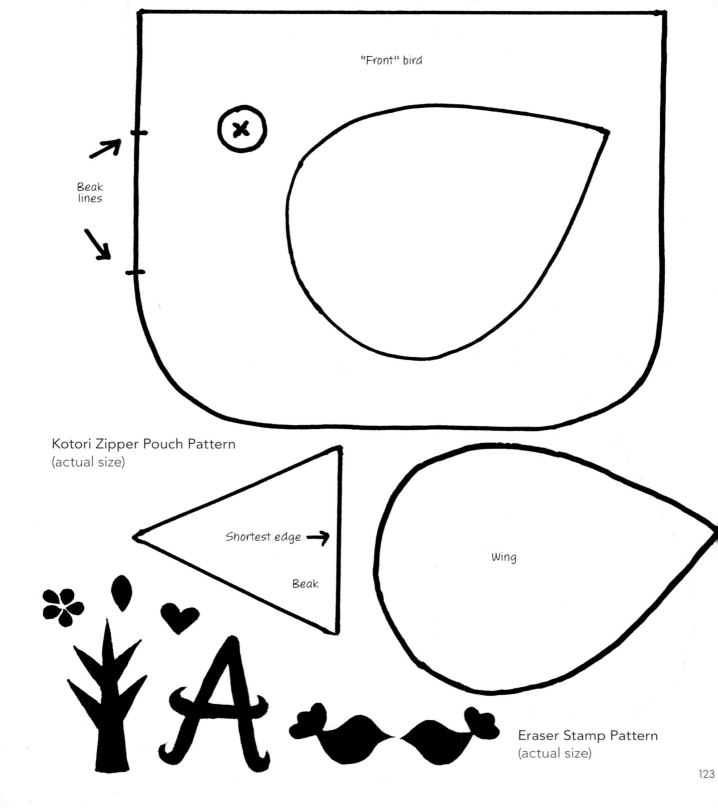

"Front" bird

Beak
lines

Kotori Zipper Pouch Pattern
(actual size)

Shortest edge →

Beak

Wing

Eraser Stamp Pattern
(actual size)

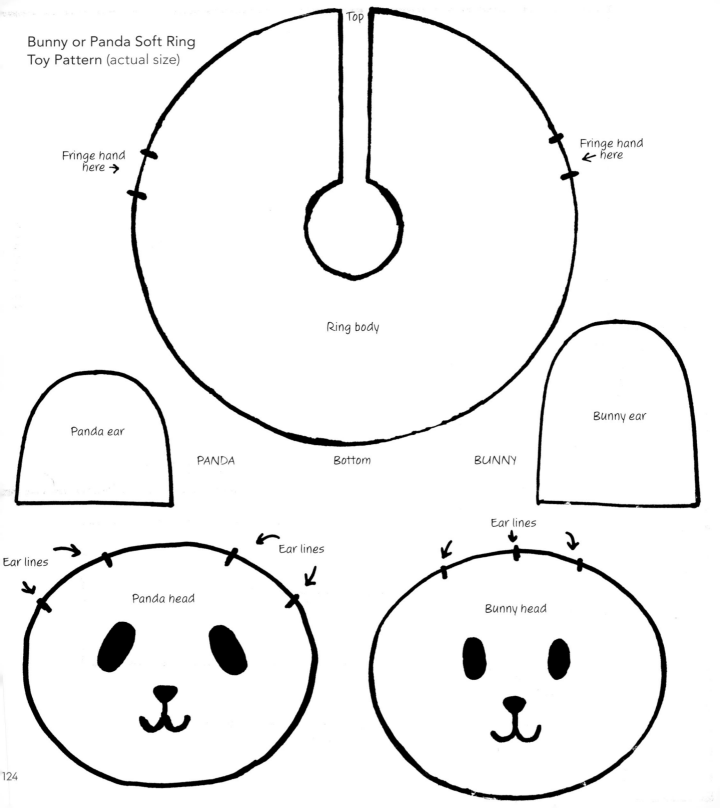

Bunny or Panda Soft Ring
Toy Pattern (actual size)

Top

Fringe hand here →

Fringe hand here

Ring body

Fringe hand here ←

Panda ear

Bunny ear

PANDA

Bottom

BUNNY

Ear lines

Ear lines

Panda head

Ear lines

Ear lines

Ear lines

Bunny head

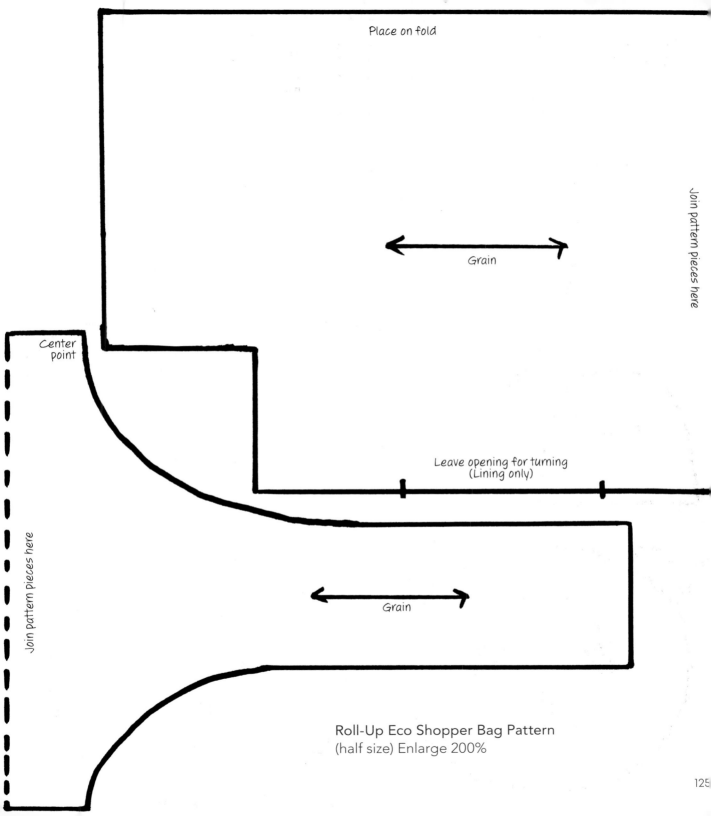

Place on fold

Join pattern pieces here

Grain

Center point

Join pattern pieces here

Leave opening for turning
(Lining only)

Grain

Roll-Up Eco Shopper Bag Pattern
(half size) Enlarge 200%

Sashiko Embroidery
Pattern (actual size)

Crochet Doily and
Linen Pouch Pattern
(actual size)

Sheep Embroidery Pattern
(actual size)

Place on fold

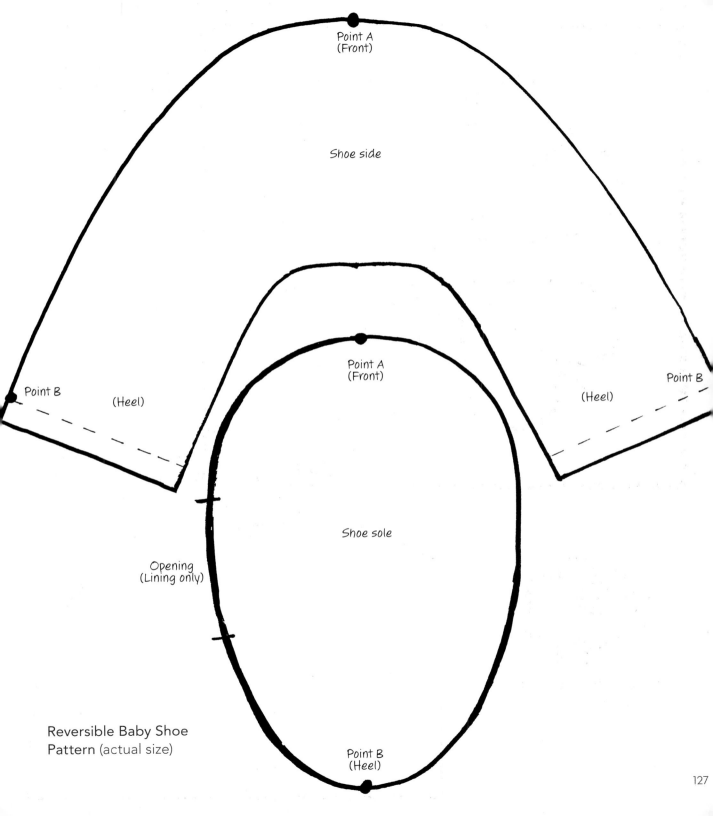

Point A
(Front)

Shoe side

Point B

(Heel)

Point B

(Heel)

Point A
(Front)

Shoe sole

Opening
(Lining only)

Reversible Baby Shoe
Pattern (actual size)

Point B
(Heel)

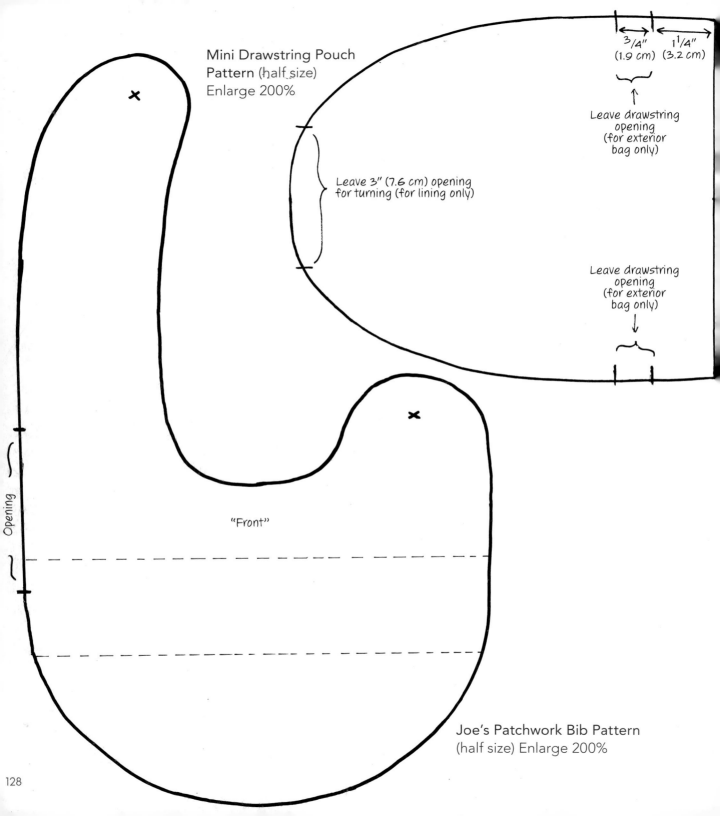

Mini Drawstring Pouch
Pattern (half size)
Enlarge 200%

3/4" (1.9 cm) 1 1/4" (3.2 cm)

Leave drawstring
opening (for exterior
bag only)

Leave 3" (7.6 cm) opening
for turning (for lining only)

Leave drawstring
opening (for exterior
bag only)

Opening

"Front"

Joe's Patchwork Bib Pattern
(half size) Enlarge 200%